SADLIER-OXFORD **LEVEL B**

Vocabulary
Workshop
Enhanced Edition

The classic program for:

- *developing* and *enhancing* vocabulary resources

- *promoting* more effective communication in today's world

- *improving* vocabulary skills assessed on standardized and/or college-admission tests

By
Jerome Shostak

D1232988

Sadlier-Oxford

A Division of William H. Sadlier, Inc.
9 Pine Street
New York, NY 10005-1002
1-800-221-5175

Contents

ISBN: 0-8215-0607-2
3456789/9876

Home Office: 9 Pine Street
New York, NY 10005-1002
1-800-221-5175

Requests for permission to make copies of any part of the work should be mailed to:

Permissions Department
William H. Sadlier, Inc.
9 Pine Street
New York, NY 10005-1002

Foreword

For close to five decades VOCABULARY WORKSHOP has been a highly successful tool for guiding and stimulating systematic vocabulary growth for students. It has also been extremely valuable for preparing students to take the types of standardized vocabulary tests commonly used to assess grade placement, competence for graduation, and/or college readiness. The *Enhanced Edition* has faithfully maintained those features that have made the program so beneficial in these two areas, while introducing new elements to keep abreast of changing times and changing standardized-test procedures, particularly the SAT. The features that make VOCABULARY WORKSHOP so valuable include:

Word List
Each book contains 300 or more basic words, selected on the basis of:
- currency in present-day usage
- frequency on recognized vocabulary lists
- applicability to standardized tests
- current grade-placement research

Units
The words in each book are organized around 15 short, stimulating *Units* featuring:
- pronunciation and parts of speech
New! - definitions—fuller treatment in the *Enhanced Edition*
- synonyms and antonyms
- usage (one phrase and two sentences)

Reviews
Five *Reviews* highlight and reinforce the work of the units through challenging exercises involving:
New! - shades of meaning (SAT-type critical-thinking exercise)
- analogies
- sentence completions
- definitions
- word families
- synonyms and antonyms

Cumulative Reviews
Four *Cumulative Reviews* utilize standardized testing techniques to provide ongoing assessment of word mastery, all involving SAT-type critical-thinking skills. Here the exercises revolve around
New! - shades of meaning
- analogies
- two-word completions

Additional Features
- A *Diagnostic Test* provides ready assessment of student needs at the outset of the term.
- The *Vocabulary of Vocabulary* reviews terms and concepts needed for effective word study.
- The *Final Mastery Test* provides end-of-term assessment of student achievement.
- *Building with Word Roots* introduces the study of etymology.
- *Enhancing Your Vocabulary,* Levels F through H, introduces students to the study of word clusters.
New! - *Working with Parts of Speech,* Levels F through H, provides further work with word clusters and introduces 50 new words per level.

Ancillary Materials
- An *Answer Key* for each level supplies answers to all materials in the student text.
- A *Series Teacher's Guide* provides a thorough overview of the features in each level, along with tips for using them effectively.
- The *Supplementary Testing Program: Cycle One, Cycle Two* provide two complete programs of separate and different testing materials for each level, so testing can be varied. A *Combined Answer Key* for each level is also available.
- The SAT-type *TEST PREP Blackline Masters* for each level provide further testing materials designed to help students prepare for SAT-type standardized tests.
- An *Interactive Audio Pronunciation Program* is also available for each level.

Pronunciation Key

The pronunciation is indicated for every basic word introduced in this book. The symbols used for this purpose, as listed below, are similar to those appearing in most standard dictionaries of recent vintage. The author has consulted a large number of dictionaries for this purpose but has relied primarily on *Webster's Third New International Dictionary* and *The Random House Dictionary of the English Language (Unabridged)*.

There are, of course, many English words for which two (or more) pronunciations are commonly accepted. In virtually all cases where such words occur in this book, the author has sought to make things easier for the student by giving just one pronunciation. The only significant exception occurs when the pronunciation changes in accordance with a shift in the part of speech. Thus we would indicate that *project* in the verb form is pronounced prə 'jekt, and in the noun form, 'präj ekt.

It is believed that these relatively simple pronunciation guides will be readily usable by the student. It should be emphasized, however, that the *best* way to learn the pronunciation of a word is to listen to and imitate an educated speaker.

Vowels

ā	lake	e	stress	ü	loot, new
a	mat	ī	knife	ů	foot, pull
â	care	i	sit	ə	rug, broken
ä	bark, bottle	ō	flow	ər	bird, better
aů	doubt	ô	all, cord		
ē	beat, wordy	oi	oil		

Consonants

ch	child, lecture	s	cellar	wh	what
g	give	sh	shun	y	yearn
j	gentle, bridge	th	thank	z	is
ŋ	sing	ŧħ	those	zh	measure

All other consonants are sounded as in the alphabet.

Stress

The accent mark *precedes* the syllable receiving the major stress: en 'rich

Parts of Speech

adj.	adjective	*int.*	interjection	*prep.*	preposition
adv.	adverb	*n.*	noun	*v.*	verb
		part.	participle		
		pl.	plural		

The Vocabulary of Vocabulary

Many valuable words are commonly used in connection with vocabulary. Knowing these words will help you organize your study of vocabulary and gain control of new words with greater ease. Some terms of this type that you should know are presented below. The exercises in each section will give you a chance to apply your knowledge of the "vocabulary of vocabulary."

Synonyms and Antonyms

Synonyms

A *synonym* is a word that has the same (or almost the same) meaning as another word.

EXAMPLES:
above—overhead   silent—noiseless
follow—pursue   try—attempt

Exercises

In each of the following groups, encircle the word that is most nearly **the same** in meaning as the first word in **boldface type**.

1. edge	**3. build**	**5. inexpensive**	**7. wish**
a. fence	a. improve	a. cheap	a. save
b. border	b. plan	b. dear	b. desire
c. corner	c. construct	c. wasteful	c. hold
d. bottom	d. play	d. worthwhile	d. shop
2. calm	**4. content**	**6. close**	**8. helper**
a. joyful	a. wealthy	a. wear	a. owner
b. sorrowful	b. dull	b. open	b. supervisor
c. still	c. excited	c. shut	c. assistant
d. upset	d. satisfied	d. remove	d. boss

Antonyms

An *antonym* is a word that is opposite (or almost opposite) in meaning to another word.

EXAMPLES: high—low   fast—slow   love—hate

Exercises

In each of the following groups, encircle the word that is most nearly **opposite** in meaning to the word in **boldface type**.

1. dull	**2. end**	**3. sorrow**	**4. reward**
a. clean	a. leave	a. joy	a. compliment
b. open	b. borrow	b. hunger	b. punish
c. interesting	c. suffer	c. anger	c. cancel
d. quiet	d. begin	d. tearfulness	d. praise

5. beautiful	**7. correct**	**9. generous**	**11. wealthy**
a. ugly	a. tall	a. mistaken	a. happy
b. female	b. bright	b. good	b. famous
c. uneducated	c. new	c. stingy	c. evil
d. useful	d. wrong	d. amusing	d. poor
6. tired	**8. hero**	**10. victorious**	**12. unite**
a. restless	a. judge	a. cowardly	a. separate
b. rested	b. villain	b. defeated	b. control
c. patient	c. actor	c. brave	c. refuse
d. arrested	d. dentist	d. penniless	d. bother

Words Pronounced Alike; Words Spelled Alike

Homonyms

A *homonym* is a word having the same (or almost the same) pronunciation as another word but a different meaning and a different spelling.

EXAMPLES: write—right   bee—be   hole—whole

Exercises

*In each of the following sentences, encircle in the parentheses the **homonym** that correctly completes the meaning.*

1. Time and (**tied, tide**) wait for no man.
2. You just (**slay, sleigh**) me with your sense of humor.
3. I told her that her (**seem, seam**) was not straight.
4. It was a (**seen, scene**) I would not have missed for the world.
5. The ball went (**through, threw**) the open window.
6. He has a heart of (**steel, steal**).
7. I was unable to (**reed, read**) what she had written.
8. If you are not careful, you will (**lose, loose**) your other glove too!
9. My kingdom for a (**hoarse, horse**).
10. Of course, I (**new, knew**) it all the time!

Homographs

A *homograph* is a word having the same spelling as another word but a different meaning.

EXAMPLE:

State may mean *to tell or say.*

Please *state* your case.

State may mean *a political unit or organization.*

There are 50 *states* in the United States.

Exercises   In Column C, write each homograph suggested by the definitions given in Columns A and B. In each case, one word will fit both definitions. The first letter of each of the missing words is given in Column C. The dashes indicate the letters to be filled in.

Column A	Column B	Column C
1. flower	ascended, went up	r _ _ _
2. unit in the alphabet	written message	l _ _ _ _ _
3. sharp blow	pleasant drink	p _ _ _ _
4. below	small feathers on a duck	d _ _ _
5. season of year	descend, go down	f _ _ _

Parts of a Word

Prefixes   A *prefix* is a syllable or syllables placed at the beginning of a word.

EXAMPLES: ex- ab- sub- pre-

Suffixes   A *suffix* is a syllable or syllables placed at the end of a word.

EXAMPLES: -ancy -or -ed -ing

Roots   A *root* or *base* is the main part of the word to which prefixes and suffixes may be added.

EXAMPLES: -tract- -ceive- -spire- -duct-

Exercises   Divide each of the following words into its prefix, root, and suffix. Some of the words may lack either a prefix, a suffix, or both. The first word has been done for you.

Word	Prefix	Root	Suffix
1. forgiveness	for	give	ness
2. describe	_____	_____	_____
3. overtake	_____	_____	_____
4. diction	_____	_____	_____
5. introduction	_____	_____	_____
6. postponed	_____	_____	_____
7. abnormal	_____	_____	_____
8. restoration	_____	_____	_____
9. deferment	_____	_____	_____
10. refrigerator	_____	_____	_____

Denotation and Connotation

Denotation The *denotation* of a word is its specific dictionary definition.

EXAMPLES:

Word	Denotation
creative	inventive, imaginative
conspiracy	a plot
measure	to find the size or amount

Connotation The *connotation* of a word is its tone—that is, the emotions or associations it normally arouses in people using, hearing, or reading it. Depending on what these feelings are, the connotation of a word may be *favorable (positive)* or *unfavorable (pejorative)*. A word that does not normally arouse strong emotions of any kind has a *neutral* connotation.

EXAMPLES:

Word	Connotation
creative	favorable
conspiracy	unfavorable
measure	neutral

Exercises *In the space provided, label the connotation of each of the following words **F** for "favorable," **U** for "unfavorable," or **N** for "neutral."*

_____ **1.** bungle   _____ **5.** amiable   _____ **9.** unerring

_____ **2.** valiant   _____ **6.** scissors   _____ **10.** illicit

_____ **3.** ingratitude   _____ **7.** wholesome   _____ **11.** bigot

_____ **4.** relate   _____ **8.** inept   _____ **12.** face

Literal and Figurative Usage

Literal Usage When a word or expression is being used in a *literal* sense, it is being employed in its strict (or primary) dictionary meaning in a situation (or *context*) that "makes sense" from a purely logical point of view.

EXAMPLE: The fencing club's emblem shows a picture of a pair of *crossed swords*.

Figurative Usage Sometimes words or expressions are used in a symbolic or nonliteral way in situations that do not "make sense" from a purely logical point of view. We call this non-literal or "extended" application of a word or expression a *figurative* or *metaphorical* usage.

EXAMPLE: Though the two Senators have *crossed swords* on more than one occasion, they like each other very much.

Exercises   *In the space provided, write **L** for "literal" or **F** for "figurative" next to each of the following sentences to show how the italicized word or expression is being used.*

_____ **1.** In my opinion, a triple-decker sandwich isn't complete without a juicy *pickle* on the side.

_____ **2.** When the leading man in our school play sprained his ankle on opening night, we knew we were really in a *pickle*.

_____ **3.** The principal stressed the importance of schooling by noting that a good education is a *gateway* to success.

_____ **4.** Mother planted a bed of tulips near the *gateway* in the fence.

Analogies

An *analogy* is a comparison. For example, we can draw an analogy, or comparison, between the human eye and a camera.

In standardized examinations you may be asked to find the relationship between two words. Then, to show that you understand the relationship, you are asked to choose another pair of words that show the same type of relationship.

EXAMPLE: **find** is to **lose** as
a. hurry is to run
b. read is to sleep
c. start is to begin
d. take is to give

Note that *find* and *lose* are opposite in meaning. Of the four choices given, which pair is made up of words that are also opposite in meaning? The answer, clearly, is *d, take is to give.*

Exercises   *Encircle the item that best completes each analogy.*

1. Ice is to **cold** as
a. steam is to cool
b. snow is to warm
c. fire is to hot
d. water is to dry

2. hollow is to **solid** as
a. simple is to easy
b. little is to tiny
c. fluid is to liquid
d. shallow is to deep

3. victim is to **accident** as
a. jury is to trial
b. casualty is to battle
c. doctor is to operation
d. prize is to game

4. brave is to **courage** as
a. sick is to health
b. faithful is to loyalty
c. sad is to happiness
d. ugly is to beauty

5. soldier is to **land** as
a. marine is to uniform
b. officer is to rank
c. sailor is to sea
d. recruit is to training

6. carpenter is to **hammer** as
a. teacher is to school
b. doctor is to bill
c. lawyer is to defendant
d. painter is to brush

Context Clues

When you do the various word-omission exercises in this book, look for *context clues* built right into the passage to guide you to the correct answer.

Restatement Clues

A *restatement* clue consists of a synonym for, or a definition of, a missing word.

EXAMPLE:

We would never have guessed that the strange-looking gadget was in fact a _____ for flipping pancakes.

a. contest   (b.) device   c. contract   d. plan

Contrast Clues

A *contrast* clue consists of an antonym for, or a phrase meaning the opposite of, a missing word.

EXAMPLE:

Off the court she is a sweet-tempered girl, but put a tennis racket in her hand and she turns into a (**veteran, ferocious**) competitor.

Situational Clues

In this type of clue, the *situation* outlined in the sentence suggests the sense of the word that is wanted but does not state its meaning directly.

EXAMPLE:

Together, our pitchers _____ nine wins, including a string of five _____ victories, to lead our team to the championship.

a. allowed . . . typical
b. batted . . . close
(c.) compiled . . . consecutive
d. dropped . . . possible

Exercises

Use context clues to choose the word or words that best complete each of the following sentences.

1. Though our troops managed to turn back the enemy's first assault, they could not hope to _____ another such attack.

a. surrender   b. withstand   c. retreat   d. relay

2. Their basketball squad does not lack for size or speed, but it is sadly (**abundant, deficient**) in teamwork and preparation.

3. To make sure that the hotel had set aside the rooms we requested, we asked them to _____ our _____ in writing.

a. cancel . . . schedule
b. demand . . . payment
c. bill . . . vacation
d. confirm . . . reservations

Diagnostic Test

This test contains a sampling of the words that are to be found in the exercises in this Vocabulary Workshop. It will give you an idea of the types and levels of the words to be studied. When you have completed all the units, the Final Mastery Test at the end of the book will assess what you have learned. By comparing your results on the Final Mastery Test with your results on the Diagnostic Test below, you will be able to judge your progress.

Synonyms   *In each of the following groups, encircle the item that most nearly expresses the meaning of the word in* **boldface type** *in the introductory phrase.*

1. interrogate the witness
a. question   b. believe   c. punish   d. listen to

2. live a **humdrum** life
a. exciting   b. poor   c. unusual   d. dull

3. insinuate that I eat too much
a. claim   b. deny   c. admit   d. imply

4. vicious animals
a. gentle   b. trained   c. savage   d. useful

5. a **customary** procedure
a. wrong   b. profitable   c. clever   d. usual

6. accused of **homicide**
a. killing   b. lying   c. stealing   d. cheating

7. lubricate the car
a. start   b. oil   c. stop   d. repair

8. a **legitimate** government
a. lawful   b. foreign   c. new   d. tyrannical

9. indulge the children
a. coddle   b. discipline   c. mistreat   d. feed

10. loom on the horizon
a. see   b. notice   c. discover   d. appear

11. miscellaneous objects
a. worthless   b. expensive   c. various   d. similar

12. an **abnormal** situation
a. typical   b. terrible   c. funny   d. unusual

13. procure assistance
a. seek   b. offer   c. reject   d. obtain

14. a **sodden** pile of leaves
a. little   b. wet   c. huge   d. messy

15. become a **fugitive**
a. criminal   b. runaway   c. jailer   d. victim

16. nothing more than a **hoax**
a. fraud   b. nobody   c. thief   d. problem

17. set **ultimate** goals
a. temporary   b. hasty   c. sincere   d. final

18. **prominent** members of our community
a. shady   b. wealthy   c. leading   d. foreign

19. **reluctant** assistants
a. experienced   b. awkward   c. unwilling   d. paid

20. an act of **vengeance**
a. mercy   b. revenge   c. daring   d. fate

21. be ever **vigilant**
a. careless   b. carefree   c. merciless   d. alert

22. bring down their **wrath**
a. troubles   b. rage   c. self-esteem   d. temperature

23. **proficient** workers
a. inexperienced   b. awkward   c. slow   d. skillful

24. **sagacious** remarks
a. nasty   b. humorous   c. kind   d. wise

25. without **prior** planning
a. earlier   b. intelligent   c. necessary   d. careful

26. **flourish** their swords
a. hold   b. seize   c. destroy   d. wave

27. a **legible** report
a. detailed   b. recent   c. readable   d. thorough

28. a highly **disputatious** person
a. likable   b. annoying   c. logical   d. argumentative

29. in a **melancholy** mood
a. typical   b. angry   c. strange   d. sad

30. **inflict** pain
a. cause   b. cure   c. study   d. fear

Antonyms   *In each of the following groups, encircle the expression that is most nearly **opposite** in meaning to the word in **boldface type** in the introductory phrase.*

31. **gigantic** tomatoes
a. ripe   b. tiny   c. poisonous   d. expensive

32. a **fruitless** effort
a. costly   b. hurried   c. successful   d. halfhearted

33. a **clarification** of the issue
a. discussion   b. avoidance   c. confusion   d. explanation

34. **ignite** a fire
a. extinguish   b. feed   c. ignore   d. report

35. very **hardy** plants
a. unusual   b. beautiful   c. fragile   d. expensive

36. a **grim** forecast
a. detailed   b. rosy   c. gloomy   d. recent

37. a **hilarious** movie
a. long   b. sad   c. profitable   d. foreign

38. **despondent** about his grades
a. overjoyed   b. careful   c. unhappy   d. concerned

39. a major **catastrophe**
a. war   b. problem   c. disaster   d. triumph

40. a truly **hospitable** welcome
a. warm   b. unexpected   c. cold   d. fitting

41. a **lavish** gift
a. costly   b. unusual   c. beautiful   d. skimpy

42. a **cluttered** room
a. spacious   b. tidy   c. carpeted   d. messy

43. **prudent** in her use of money
a. foolish   b. stingy   c. thoughtful   d. wise

44. **hostile** actions
a. sensitive   b. friendly   c. cheerful   d. unusual

45. voiced **trivial** objections to the plan
a. silly   b. significant   c. several   d. separate

46. an unexpected **surplus** of wheat
a. harvest   b. demand   c. use   d. lack

47. **vital** to our well-being
a. important   b. sympathetic   c. unnecessary   d. accustomed

48. a **graphic** account
a. partial   b. vivid   c. long-winded   d. colorless

49. very **lax** about discipline
a. unconcerned   b. happy   c. strict   d. forgetful

50. feel very **lethargic** today
a. energetic   b. gloomy   c. tired   d. confident

Unit 1

Note carefully the spelling, pronunciation, and definition of each of the following words. Then write the word in the blank space in the illustrative phrase following.

1. adjacent
(ə 'jās ənt)

(*adj.*) near, next to, adjoining

Boston and its _____ suburbs

2. alight
(ə 'līt)

(*v.*) to get down from, step down from; to come down from the air, land; (*adj.*) lighted up

_____ from the plane

3. barren
('bar ən)

(*adj.*) not productive, bare

a _____ landscape

4. disrupt
(dis 'rəpt)

(*v.*) to break up, disturb

_____ the meeting

5. dynasty
('dī nə stē)

(*n.*) a powerful family or group of rulers that maintains its position or power for some time

the Han _____ of China

6. foretaste
('fôr tāst)

(*n.*) an advance indication, sample, or warning

a _____ of things to come

7. germinate
('jər mə nāt)

(*v.*) to begin to grow, come into being

let thoughts _____ in one's mind

8. humdrum
('həm drəm)

(*adj.*) ordinary, dull, routine, without variation

_____ household tasks

9. hurtle
('hər təl)

(*v.*) to rush violently, dash headlong; to fling or hurl forcefully

_____ through space

10. insinuate
(in 'sin yü āt)

(*v.*) to suggest or hint slyly; to edge into something indirectly

_____ that something is false

11. interminable
(in 'tər mə nə bəl)

(*adj.*) endless, so long as to seem endless

an _____ wait

12. interrogate
(in 'ter ə gāt)

(*v.*) to ask questions, examine by questioning

_____ the suspect

13. recompense
('rek əm pens)

(*v.*) to pay back, give a reward; (*n.*) a payment for loss, service, or injury

_____ her for her time and effort

14. renovate
('ren ə vāt)

(*v.*) to repair, restore to good condition, make new again

_____ the old house

15. résumé
('rez ə mā)

(*n.*) a brief summary; a short written account of one's education, working experience, or qualifications for a job

prepare a _____ of their findings

16. sullen
('səl ən)

(*adj.*) silent or brooding because of ill humor, anger, or resentment; slow moving, sluggish

a _____ crowd

17. trickle
('trik əl)

(*v.*) to flow or fall by drops or in a small stream;
(*n.*) a small, irregular quantity of anything

a _____ of water from the pipe

18. trivial
('triv ē əl)

(*adj.*) not important, minor; ordinary, commonplace

_____ details

19. truce
(trüs)

(*n.*) a pause in fighting, temporary peace

agree to a five-day _____

20. vicious
('vish əs)

(*adj.*) evil, bad; spiteful; having bad habits or an ugly disposition; painfully severe or extreme

a _____ rumor

Completing the Sentence

Choose the word from this unit that best completes each of the following sentences. Write the word in the space provided.

1. She was so happy and grateful that I felt more than _____ for all that I had tried to do to help her.

2. In only a few days, the seeds that I had planted in the fertile soil of the garden began to _____ and take root.

3. Cleaning up after the big party, which was supposed to take "just a few minutes," proved to be an almost _____ job.

4. As the drought continued without a letup, the once fertile farmlands of the region slowly became _____ "dust bowls."

5. The judge said to the lawyer, "You have a right to _____ the witness, but there is no need to bully her."

6. Though my dog Rover is huge and fierce-looking, children are fond of him because he doesn't have a(n) _____ disposition.

7. Although they lived in a house _____ to ours, we never really got to know them well.

8. Many people who lead rather _____ lives get a great thrill from watching the exciting adventures of TV and movie superheroes.

9. I never would have thought that so bitter and long-lasting a quarrel could result from such a(n) _____ and unimportant cause.

10. As we sat at the side of the lake, we enjoyed watching the wild geese swoop down and _____ on the surface of the water.

11. We need large sums of money to keep our school system going, but we are getting only a(n) _____ of funds from the state.

12. Although the building is old and needs repair, we are convinced that we can _____ it without spending a lot of money.

13. The suspect's only reaction to the detective's question was a wry smile and _____ silence.

14. After the warring nations had agreed to a(n) _____ , they faced the far more difficult task of working out a real peace.

15. When I applied for the job, I left a(n) _____ of my previous work experience with the personnel office.

16. In the 11th century, a foreign warlord invaded the country and set up a(n) _____ that ruled for more than 250 years.

17. Though they didn't say so in so many words, they did _____ that I was responsible for the accident.

18. The "coming attractions" shown before the main feature gave us a distinct _____ of what the next feature would be like.

19. Our carefully laid plans were completely _____ by a sudden and totally unexpected turn of events.

20. At that moment, Helen lost control of the car, and it _____ off the road into a clump of bushes.

Synonyms   *Choose the word from this unit that is most nearly **the same** in meaning as each of the following groups of expressions. Write the word on the line given.*

1. payment, compensation; to repay   _____

2. monotonous, uneventful, prosaic; boring   _____

3. wicked, evil; malicious; savage   _____

4. to repair, fix up, recondition   _____

5. to question, query, examine   _____

6. endless, never-ending, ceaseless   _____

7. grumpy, surly, peevish, morose   _____

8. to dismount, descend; to land, touch down _____

9. to upset, disturb, displace, disorder _____

10. to hint at, imply; to edge into _____

11. next to, alongside, nearby _____

12. a summary, synopsis; a job history _____

13. a cease-fire, armistice _____

14. unproductive, sterile; desolate, arid _____

15. a preview, anticipation _____

16. to speed, fly, race, catapult; to fling _____

17. insignificant, petty, trifling _____

18. a small amount; to dribble, drizzle, drip _____

19. a ruling house, regime _____

20. to sprout, shoot up, grow, burgeon _____

Antonyms *Choose the word from this unit that is most nearly* **opposite** *in meaning to each of the following groups of expressions. Write the word on the line given.*

1. good; kind, kindly; mild, harmless _____

2. to crawl, creep _____

3. fertile, productive, fruitful _____

4. cheerful, blithe, sociable, vivacious _____

5. to wither, die, stagnate, shrivel up _____

6. to gush, pour, flood; a deluge _____

7. to mount, ascend, board; to take off _____

8. lively, exciting, thrilling, exhilarating _____

9. faraway, distant, remote _____

10. brief, short, fleeting _____

11. important, weighty, momentous _____

12. to put in order, organize _____

13. war, warfare, fighting _____

14. to speak one's mind plainly; to barge in _____

15. to let something go to wrack and ruin _____

14

1. When we are having fun, time rushes by, but even five minutes in the dentist's waiting room may seem (**adjacent, interminable**).

2. I am angry not because she criticized me but because she made remarks that were untrue and (**trivial, vicious**).

3. When I saw a big "A" on my term paper in English, I felt that I had been fully (**germinated, recompensed**) for all my hours of hard work.

4. The way to be successful at a job is to carry out all instructions carefully, even though you think some of them are (**trivial, sullen**) or silly.

5. The administration had no major scandals, but it was also (**barren, sullen**) of outstanding accomplishments.

6. Planted in the fertile soil of her imagination, the seed of a great idea soon (**germinated, disrupted**) into a workable proposal.

7. Regardless of who started this silly quarrel, isn't it time for us to declare a (**dynasty, truce**) and work together for the best interests of the school?

8. Even the most (**humdrum, vicious**) work can be interesting if you regard it as a challenge to do the very best you can.

9. As he grew old, the torrent of beautiful music that he had produced for so many years was reduced to a mere (**foretaste, trickle**).

10. Our team spirit is so high that there is never a (**sullen, trivial**) reaction from players who aren't chosen to start a game.

11. The principal asked the students not to "hang around" in front of the houses and other buildings (**adjacent to, alighting**) the school.

12. Are we going to allow minor disagreements to (**disrupt, recompense**) the club that we have worked so hard to organize?

13. With only a few seconds left to play, our fullback (**hurtled, insinuated**) over the line and scored the winning touchdown.

14. What we want to do is (**recompense, renovate**) the old house without harming its charm and beauty.

15. The stewardess asked the passengers to make sure that they had all their personal belongings before (**disrupting, alighting**) from the aircraft.

16. He said that he was going to ask only "a few casual questions," but I soon saw that he wanted to (**recompense, interrogate**) me thoroughly.

17. "The program the usher handed you contains a brief (**résumé, dynasty**) of the action of the opera you are about to see," I replied.

18. With flattery and clever half-truths, the newcomers (**insinuated, renovated**) themselves into the inner circle of the organization.

19. If the sights we've seen today are a true (**recompense, foretaste**) of what lies ahead, we're in for some real treats.

20. For three generations, the Barrymore family has formed one of the leading theatrical (**truces, dynasties**) of this country.

Unit 2

Definitions

Note carefully the spelling, pronunciation, and definition of each of the following words. Then write the word in the blank space in the illustrative phrase following.

1. **available**
   (ə ′vā lə bəl)

   (*adj.*) ready for use, at hand

   made the office _____

2. **cater**
   (′kā tər)

   (*v.*) to satisfy the needs of, try to make things easy and pleasant; to supply food and service

   _____ to all their whims

3. **customary**
   (′kəs tə mer ē)

   (*adj.*) usual, expected, routine

   the _____ reward

4. **dissuade**
   (dis ′wād)

   (*v.*) to persuade not to do something

   _____ them from quitting

5. **entrepreneur**
   (än trə prə ′nər)

   (*n.*) a person who starts up and takes on the risk of a business

   a magazine for _____

6. **firebrand**
   (′fī ər brand)

   (*n.*) a piece of burning wood; a troublemaker; an extremely energetic or emotional person

   a rash young _____

7. **hazard**
   (′haz ərd)

   (*n.*) risk, peril; (*v.*) to expose to danger or harm; to gamble

   the _____ of driving

8. **homicide**
   (′hom ə cīd)

   (*n.*) the killing of one person by another

   guilty of _____

9. **indifference**
   (in ′dif rəns)

   (*n.*) a lack of interest or concern

   a matter of complete _____ to me

10. **indignant**
    (in ′dig nənt)

    (*adj.*) filled with resentment or anger over something unjust, unworthy, or mean

    an _____ letter to the editor

11. **indispensable**
    (in di ′spen sə bəl)

    (*adj.*) absolutely necessary, not to be neglected

    _____ to life

12. **lubricate**
    (′lü brə kāt)

    (*v.*) to apply oil or grease; to make smooth, slippery, or easier to use

    _____ the machinery regularly

13. **mutual**
    (′myü chü əl)

    (*adj.*) shared, felt, or shown equally by two or more

    a _____ admiration society

14. **pelt**
    (pelt)

    (*v.*) to throw a stream of things; to strike successively; to hurry

    _____ the car with snowballs

15. plague
(plāg)

(*n.*) an easily spread disease causing a large number of deaths; a widespread evil; (*v.*) to annoy or bother

a _____ spread by rats

16. poised
(poizd)

(*adj., part.*) balanced, suspended; calm, controlled; ready for action

_____ for takeoff

17. regime
(rā 'zhēm)

(*n.*) a government in power; a form or system of rule or management; a period of rule

the present _____ in Chile

18. retard
(ri 'tärd)

(*v.*) to make slow, delay, hold back

_____ progress

19. transparent
(trans 'par ənt)

(*adj.*) allowing light to pass through; easily recognized or understood; easily seen through or detected

a _____ glass door

20. unscathed
(ən 'skāthd)

(*adj.*) wholly unharmed, not injured

emerged _____ from the wreck

Completing the Sentence

Choose the word from this unit that best completes each of the following sentences. Write the word in the space provided.

1. Angry at the call, the crowd began to _____ the referee with all kinds of refuse.

2. At the front desk, a(n) _____ guest was angrily complaining about the shabby treatment he had received from the staff of the hotel.

3. Since the seat covers in the car were _____ , we could see the attractive pattern of the upholstery underneath.

4. No one has ever been able to explain to my satisfaction how Indian holy men can walk _____ across beds of hot coals.

5. Most of the homeowners in this area have tried in vain to overcome the _____ of crabgrass that threatens to overrun their lawns.

6. When we _____ a car, we try to cut down the friction at every point where one surface rubs against another.

7. Until it was almost too late, the hunters did not see the leopard crouching in a tree, _____ to leap on them.

8. Having spent many years as political opponents, the two Congressmen have developed a(n) _____ respect for each other.

9. The guidance counselor tried to _____ me from taking the job because she thought the work would be too pressured for me.

10. Although we arrived at the stadium a few minutes before game time, we found that many good seats were still _____ .

11. A sense of humor is _____ if you are to cope with all the strains and difficulties of everyday life.

12. With the emergence of market economies in Eastern Europe have come flocks of _____ seeking business opportunities there.

13. Mother prepares wholesome, tasty meals, but she says she is not going to _____ to the special tastes of six different children.

14. When the wounded shopkeeper died, the charges against the person who had been arrested were raised from robbery to _____ .

15. Though they have done nothing to hasten passage of the bill, they haven't tried to _____ the process either.

16. Eventually the army toppled the country's democratic _____ and set up a military dictatorship in its place.

17. Only a really hard-hearted person could show such _____ to the plight of the homeless who wander our streets.

18. Though the habit of taking a siesta in the afternoon may seem strange to a foreigner, it is quite _____ in this part of the world.

19. It takes a special kind of bravery to face the _____ of life in the jungle.

20. It took the authorities quite some time to put down the riot that a few rash _____ had managed to start.

Synonyms   *Choose the word from this unit that is most nearly **the same** in meaning as each of the following groups of expressions. Write the word on the line given.*

1. offended, resentful, outraged, exasperated   _____

2. businessperson, impresario   _____

3. essential, crucial, vital   _____

4. manslaughter, murder   _____

5. two-sided, joint, shared, reciprocal   _____

6. to bombard, shower, pepper   _____

7. clear, translucent; obvious   _____

8. a hothead, agitator, rabble-rouser   _____

9. an epidemic, pestilence; to pester, vex _____

10. to oil, grease _____

11. to pamper, indulge, gratify; to provide _____

12. a danger, risk; to venture _____

13. unhurt, sound, intact, unimpaired _____

14. a lack of interest, apathy, unconcern _____

15. to hold back, slow down, restrain _____

16. a government, administration, rule _____

17. obtainable; on hand, at hand _____

18. to discourage, talk out of _____

19. calm, collected, self-confident; ready _____

20. regular, normal, usual, traditional _____

Antonyms   Choose the word from this unit that is most nearly **opposite** in meaning to each of the following groups of expressions. Write the word on the line given.

1. pleased, delighted, overjoyed, elated _____

2. injured, damaged, harmed, hurt _____

3. to frustrate, deny, refuse _____

4. one-sided, unilateral _____

5. unnecessary, nonessential _____

6. frosted; sooty, smoky; unclear, indistinct _____

7. to persuade, talk into _____

8. strange, odd, unusual, untraditional _____

9. interest, concern, enthusiasm _____

10. nervous, tense, ill at ease _____

11. unobtainable, not to be had _____

12. to hasten, speed up _____

13. a peacemaker, pacifier, conciliator _____

14. to play it safe _____

15. a boon, blessing, godsend _____

2

Choosing the Right Word   *Encircle the **boldface** word that more satisfactorily completes each of the following sentences.*

1. Your excuse for missing practice was so (**transparent, indispensable**) that even a child would have seen right through it.

2. Innocent or guilty, no one involved in a major political scandal ever comes away from it entirely (**dissuaded, unscathed**).

3. In Shakespeare's day, an actor who displeased the audience might find himself (**poised, pelted**) with a barrage of rotten vegetables.

4. A little courtesy can do much to (**dissuade, lubricate**) the machinery of our everyday social life.

5. The aid that we have (**indignantly, mutually**) given each other over the years has enabled both of us to overcome many problems.

6. All during that nightmarish period, I found myself (**plagued, dissuaded**) by doubts and fears about the future.

7. You cannot ignore me for months on end and then take it for granted that I will be (**available, customary**) whenever you want me.

8. When the salesclerk replied rudely to my polite inquiry about the price of the garment, I became a bit (**transparent, indignant**).

9. It seems that only last year she was an awkward child, but now she is a charming and (**poised, unscathed**) young woman.

10. Southern (**firebrands, hazards**) agitating for a complete break with the Union helped speed the coming of the Civil War.

11. Modern medicine has found that certain "wonder drugs" are very effective means of (**catering, retarding**) or arresting the spread of some diseases.

12. Since I am a creature of habit, I find that I can't do anything in the morning without first having my (**customary, mutual**) cup of coffee.

13. Though I have no means of knowing for sure where they happen to be, may I (**hazard, lubricate**) the guess that they're in the gym?

14. Unfortunately, nothing any of us said could (**dissuade, cater**) Ned from his plan to quit school.

15. When my 8-year-old sister started up a chain of lemonade stands, I knew we had a budding (**entrepreneur, firebrand**) in the family.

16. When the new (**hazard, regime**) took power, it canceled or reversed most of the policies of its predecessor.

17. The judge explained to the jury that killing someone in self-defense may be considered justifiable, or noncriminal, (**homicide, plague**).

18. Do you agree with the criticism that many television programs shamelessly (**cater, retard**) to the lowest tastes?

19. The (**indifference, hazard**) of Americans to government is so great that more than 40 percent of them do not even bother to vote.

20. On our long camping trip, we learned that we could get along without many things that we had considered (**indispensable, indifferent**).

Unit 3

Definitions

Note carefully the spelling, pronunciation, and definition of each of the following words. Then write the word in the blank space in the illustrative phrase following.

1. animated
('an ə māt id)

(*adj.*) full of life, lively, alive; (*part.*) moved to action

in an _____ mood

2. brood
(brüd)

(*n.*) a family of young animals, especially birds; any group having the same nature and origin; (*v.*) to think over in a worried, unhappy way

_____ over one's misfortunes

3. culminate
('kəl mə nāt)

(*v.*) to reach a high point of development; to end, climax

_____ in disaster

4. downright
('daůn rīt)

(*adv.*) thoroughly; (*adj.*) absolute, complete; frank, blunt

a _____ lie

5. drone
(drōn)

(*n.*) a loafer, idler; a buzzing or humming sound; a remote-control device; a male bee; (*v.*) to make a buzzing sound; to speak in a dull tone of voice

the _____ of the engine

6. goad
(gōd)

(*v.*) to drive or urge on; (*n.*) something used to drive or urge on

_____ them into action

7. indulge
(in 'dəlj)

(*v.*) to give in to a wish or desire, give oneself up to

_____ in self-pity

8. ingredient
(in 'grē dē ənt)

(*n.*) one of the materials in a mixture, recipe, or formula

mix the _____ in a bowl

9. literate
('lit ə rət)

(*adj.*) able to read and write; showing an excellent educational background; having knowledge or training

a highly _____ young woman

10. loom
(lüm)

(*v.*) to come into view; to appear in exaggerated form; (*n.*) a machine for weaving

the dangers that _____ ahead

11. luster
('ləs tər)

(*n.*) the quality of giving off light, brightness, glitter, brilliance

shone with a starry _____

12. miscellaneous
(mis ə 'lā nē əs)

(*adj.*) mixed, of different kinds

a collection of _____ items

13. oration
(ô 'rā shən)

(*n.*) a public speech for a formal occasion

one of Cicero's _____

14. peevish
('pē vish)

(*adj.*) cross, complaining, irritable; contrary

became _____ when hungry

15. seethe
(sēth)

(*v.*) to boil or foam; to be excited or disturbed

_____ with excitement

16. singe
(sinj)

(*v.*) to burn slightly; (*n.*) a burn at the ends or edges

accidentally _____ her eyebrows

17. unique
(yü 'nēk)

(*adj.*) one of a kind; unequaled; unusual; found only in a given class, place, or situation

a _____ situation

18. upright
('əp rīt)

(*adj.*) vertical, straight; good, honest; (*adv.*) in a vertical position

in an _____ position

19. verify
('ver ə fī)

(*v.*) to establish the truth or accuracy of, confirm

_____ the statement

20. yearn
(yərn)

(*v.*) to have a strong and earnest desire

_____ to see old friends again

Completing the Sentence

Choose the word from this unit that best completes each of the following sentences. Write it in the space given.

1. We put supports around the tree that had been partially uprooted by the storm, and it was soon standing _____ again.

2. Like some storm-tossed sea, her inventive brain _____ with all kinds of new and imaginative answers to old problems and questions.

3. When I saw how handsome my father looked in his brand-new jacket, I _____ for one exactly like it.

4. Larry has the _____ distinction of being the only student in our school ever to win varsity letters in four sports.

5. Many immigrants to the United States who cannot read and write English are _____ in their native languages.

6. The first mark of a good cook is the ability to choose the best possible _____ for the dishes he or she will prepare.

7. The Fourth of July _____ will be delivered in City Square by the Congressman from our district.

8. I believe in being careful, but Dan is _____ miserly when it comes to spending money.

9. "You're just supposed to _____ the meat," I shouted at him in dismay, "not burn it to a crisp!"

10. The dull conversation became much more _____ when it turned to a subject in which we were all interested.

11. The sunlight shining on her beautiful, copper-colored hair gave it an almost metallic _____ .

12. Indian elephant keepers usually use a short wooden _____ to control and direct the movements of their huge charges.

13. The man was the prime suspect in the crime until two eyewitnesses came forward to _____ his alibi.

14. I'm normally fairly even-tempered, but I can become _____ and irritable when I'm tired or frustrated.

15. The resentment of the American colonists against the harsh policies of the British government _____ in armed rebellion.

16. Those books which do not fit logically under any of the subjects indicated will be placed in a group labeled _____ .

17. Like the traffic guard at a school crossing, the mother hen directed her large _____ across the yard toward a torn sack of feed.

18. When storm clouds _____ on the horizon, we hurried to find shelter.

19. How pleasant it is for us city dwellers to smell the new-mown hay and listen to the _____ of bees in the clover patch!

20. I don't know which is worse—parents who are too strict with their children or parents who _____ them too much.

Synonyms   *Choose the word from this unit that is most nearly **the same** in meaning as each of the following groups of expressions. Write the word on the line given.*

1. an element, component, constituent, factor   _____

2. to emerge, surface, appear, hover, tower   _____

3. to scorch, char, sear   _____

4. to end, conclude, terminate, climax   _____

5. varied, assorted, motley   _____

6. to oblige, humor; to coddle, pamper   _____

7. perpendicular, vertical; honest, virtuous   _____

8. educated, trained, able to read and write   _____

3

9. total, out-and-out, unqualified _____

10. unparalleled, distinctive, singular _____

11. to boil, churn, foam _____

12. a formal speech or address, harangue _____

13. to prove, confirm, validate, substantiate _____

14. to ponder, meditate; to worry, agonize _____

15. a loafer; to hum, buzz, purr _____

16. crabby, cranky, testy; stubborn _____

17. to crave, long for, desire, want _____

18. gloss, sheen, brilliance _____

19. lively, energetic, vigorous _____

20. to prod, urge, spur on, incite _____

Antonyms   *Choose the word from this unit that is most nearly* ***opposite*** *in meaning to each of the following groups of expressions. Write the word on the line given.*

1. to begin, initiate, kick off, commence _____

2. to curb, check, restrain _____

3. agreeable, amiable, even-tempered, pleasant _____

4. a hard worker, workaholic _____

5. horizontal, prone; dishonest, corrupt _____

6. unlettered, unschooled, ignorant _____

7. ordinary, commonplace, run-of-the-mill _____

8. to have no desire for _____

9. dull, lifeless, dead, flat _____

10. to deny, refuse _____

11. to disprove, refute, discredit _____

12. identical, uniform, homogeneous _____

13. tarnish, dullness _____

14. to be calm and placid _____

15. to burn to a crisp, incinerate _____

Choosing the Right Word   *Encircle the **boldface** word that more satisfactorily completes each of the following sentences.*

1. An important (**ingredient, oration**) of what is commonly called luck is the willingness to take chances when an opportunity appears.

2. The (**luster, loom**) of her reputation as a friend of humanity has grown brighter with the years.

3. Though the colonies long (**seethed, singed**) with resentment at the British, the caldron of their discontent did not boil over into rebellion until 1776.

4. Even those who do not like New York must admit that it is a truly (**unique, literate**) city, quite unlike any other in the world.

5. This magazine is published not for a mass circulation but for a very small audience of highly (**peevish, literate**) people.

6. Probably no (**oration, miscellany**) in American history is so well known and loved as Lincoln's address on the battlefield of Gettysburg.

7. By Friday afternoon, all of us were (**indulging, yearning**) for the weekend.

8. The man was not just "a little careless" in handling the club's funds; he was (**downright, upright**) dishonest!

9. Modern scientists often try to (**loom, verify**) their ideas and theories by conducting extensive experiments in their laboratories.

10. "If you choose to play with fire," I warned them, "you run the risk of (**animating, singeing**) your fingers."

11. I have my doubts about people who spend too much time telling the world how noble and (**upright, downright**) they are.

12. The American people must take action right now to deal with the pollution problem that (**looms, seethes**) so large on our horizons.

13. The last thing I heard before falling asleep was the (**goad, drone**) of their voices as they continued their endless discussion of politics.

14. You may make friends very easily, but if you continue to be so (**peevish, upright**), you aren't going to keep them long.

15. Instead of (**droning, brooding**) about the misfortunes that have befallen you, why don't you go out and do something to correct the situation?

16. In his many years in Congress, he has been (**animated, culminated**) mainly by a strong desire to help the underdogs in our society.

17. It's all right for us to disagree, but let's argue about the facts only, without (**indulging, yearning**) in name-calling.

18. Each year the professional football season (**culminates, broods**) in the Superbowl game between the champions of the two conferences.

19. Neither threats nor force will (**indulge, goad**) me into doing something that in my heart I know is wrong.

20. Glenn has such a store of (**miscellaneous, upright**) information in his head that we have nicknamed him "The Encyclopedia"!

Review Units 1–3

Analogies *In each of the following, encircle the item that best completes the comparison.*

1. loom is to **weaver** as
a. role is to actor
b. press is to printer
c. horse is to rider
d. article is to writer

2. unscathed is to **injury** as
a. literate is to knowledge
b. wise is to intelligence
c. penniless is to wealth
d. celebrated is to position

3. poised is to **favorable** as
a. animated is to unfavorable
b. vicious is to favorable
c. peevish is to unfavorable
d. sullen is to favorable

4. interminable is to **end** as
a. unique is to parallel
b. indispensable is to use
c. adjacent is to vicinity
d. miscellaneous is to variety

5. hurtle is to **fast** as
a. plod is to slow
b. trudge is to fast
c. scamper is to slow
d. creep is to fast

6. trickle is to **little** as
a. gush is to much
b. deluge is to little
c. drizzle is to much
d. flood is to little

7. indifferent is to **interest** as
a. poised is to control
b. sullen is to silence
c. humdrum is to excitement
d. upright is to honesty

8. lubricate is to **oil** as
a. start is to brake
b. polish is to wax
c. stop is to gas
d. drive is to engine

9. gambler is to **hazard** as
a. banker is to waste
b. spendthrift is to husband
c. thief is to invest
d. miser is to stockpile

10. mutual is to **two** as
a. adjacent is to three
b. literate is to five
c. unique is to one
d. barren is to four

11. murderer is to **homicide** as
a. thief is to robbery
b. villain is to cheating
c. burglar is to forgery
d. liar is to smuggling

12. indignant is to **anger** as
a. vicious is to boredom
b. sullen is to resentment
c. indifferent is to concern
d. poised is to fear

13. luster is to **shine** as
a. tarnish is to gleam
b. foretaste is to twinkle
c. glamour is to seethe
d. splendor is to dazzle

14. bee is to **drone** as
a. fly is to screech
b. ant is to hum
c. cricket is to chirp
d. beetle is to hoot

15. illiterate is to **read** as
a. dumb is to hear
b. blind is to see
c. deaf is to write
d. crippled is to speak

16. singe is to **fire** as
a. toast is to coffee
b. evaporate is to milk
c. broil is to juice
d. dampen is to water

17. goad is to **elephant** as
a. crop is to horse
b. spur is to boot
c. collar is to neck
d. key is to lock

18. firebrand is to **kindle** as
a. spoilsport is to yearn
b. pickpocket is to insinuate
c. peacemaker is to extinguish
d. showoff is to hide

Synonyms   *In each of the following groups, encircle the word or expression that is most nearly* **the same** *in meaning as the* **boldface word** *in the introductory phrase.*

1. a totally **barren** wasteland
a. useful   b. dangerous   c. desolate   d. unknown

2. charged with **homicide**
a. cruelty   b. theft   c. murder   d. forgery

3. lubricate the axle of the car
a. replace   b. damage   c. repair   d. grease

4. an **upright** member of our organization
a. new   b. honest   c. famous   d. poor

5. brood about my illness
a. talk   b. think   c. ask   d. complain

6. indispensable equipment
a. costly   b. necessary   c. worthless   d. well-made

7. renovate the gymnasium
a. decorate   b. fix up   c. divide   d. enlarge

8. interrogate a witness
a. question   b. jail   c. find   d. try

9. pelt with snowballs
a. arrive   b. build   c. shower   d. fill

10. made of simple **ingredients**
a. answers   b. designs   c. elements   d. remarks

11. hurt by their **indifference**
a. unconcern   b. remark   c. bitterness   d. cruelty

12. singe her eyebrows
a. dye   b. shape   c. shave   d. burn

13. goad them to superhuman efforts
a. drive   b. restrain   c. inspire   d. steer

14. humdrum tasks
a. exciting   b. strenuous   c. difficult   d. routine

15. declared the **truce** in effect
a. law   b. treaty   c. armistice   d. plan

16. customary procedure
a. old-fashioned   b. usual   c. new   d. unusual

Shades of Meaning   *Read each sentence carefully. Then encircle the item that best completes the statement below the sentence.*

The fact that many species — including the kangaroo and platypus — are unique to Australia is due to its isolation from other continents.   **(2)**

1. In line 2 the phrase **unique to** most nearly means
a. unparalleled in   c. found only in
b. unequaled in   d. distinctive in

At the height of the Cuban missile crisis, in October 1962, the world
seemed poised on the brink of full-scale nuclear war. **(2)**

2. The word **poised** in line 2 is best defined as
a. calm
c. controlled
b. suspended
d. collected

Though in looks the twins cannot be told apart, in temperament they could
not be more different — one as meek as a lamb, the other as peevish **(2)**
as a mule.

3. In line 2 the word **peevish** is used to mean
a. obstinate
c. complaining
b. irritable
d. cross

Although the vicious headaches known as migraines have been known to
medicine for centuries, their cause is still unknown. **(2)**

4. The word **vicious** in line 1 most nearly means
a. spiteful
b. malicious
c. evil
d. severe

The boss's downright manner does not sit well with some; but I, for one,
find his frankness downright refreshing. **(2)**

5. In line 1 the word **downright** is used to mean
a. blunt
b. absolute
c. complete
d. unqualified

Antonyms   In each of the following groups, encircle the word or
expression that is most nearly **opposite** in meaning to
the **boldface word** in the introductory phrase.

1. trivial problem
a. new
b. puzzling
c. important
d. minor

2. vicious remarks
a. bitter
b. inaccurate
c. nasty
d. kind

3. interminable task
a. pleasant
b. unimportant
c. difficult
d. brief

4. lost some of its **luster**
a. value
b. dullness
c. appeal
d. glow

5. miscellaneous party favors
a. valuable
b. similar
c. colorful
d. used

6. transparent waters
a. muddy
b. clear
c. drinkable
d. dangerous

7. peevish behavior
a. irritable
b. agreeable
c. snobbish
d. puzzling

8. verify the accusation
a. read
b. confirm
c. disprove
d. type

9. animated conversation
a. lively
b. dull
c. well-informed
d. unpleasant

10. retard growth
a. hold back   b. speed up   c. account for   d. observe

11. in an **adjacent** room
a. nearby   b. well-lit   c. remote   d. stuffy

12. sullen mood
a. strange   b. ugly   c. thoughtful   d. sociable

13. unique contribution
a. commonplace   b. matchless   c. modern   d. popular

14. indignant reply
a. delighted   b. long   c. offended   d. sleepy

15. culminated in disaster
a. organized   b. began   c. announced   d. ended

Completing the Sentence

From the following words, choose the one that best completes each of the sentences below. Write the word in the space provided.

Group A

luster	**alight**	**mutual**	**plague**
loom	**cater**	**dynasty**	**upright**
recompense	**hurtle**	**firebrand**	**pelt**

1. Because Jane has always been _____ in her dealings with everyone, she now enjoys an excellent reputation.
2. As the poor fellow left the dance floor, he suddenly tripped over his own feet and _____ into the refreshment booth.
3. It will be to our _____ advantage to rent a car and share the expenses of the trip to Chicago.
4. When the speaker finished his talk, he was _____ with a barrage of questions from every corner of the huge hall.
5. Nothing we may say now can add to the _____ of her remarkable accomplishments.

Group B

literate	**unscathed**	**truce**	**germinate**
oration	**available**	**indulge**	**yearn**
résumé	**seethe**	**drone**	**regime**

1. Let's call a(n) _____ in this silly quarreling and do whatever is necessary to get the car started.
2. "Friends, Romans, countrymen, lend me your ears" are the opening words of the famous funeral _____ delivered by Mark Antony.

3. Although I see that you are _____ with impatience, I will not let you go until you give a full explanation of your conduct.

4. We must make use of every _____ pair of hands to get the gym ready for the Senior Prom.

5. Though most of the parents I know love their children very much, they wisely refuse to _____ their every whim.

Word Families

A. *On the line provided, write a **noun form** of each of the following words.*

EXAMPLE: culminate — **culmination**

1. transparent   _____

2. renovate   _____

3. cater   _____

4. unique   _____

5. insinuate   _____

6. yearn   _____

7. indulge   _____

8. vicious   _____

9. literate   _____

10. indignant   _____

11. trivial   _____

12. verify   _____

13. lubricate   _____

14. germinate   _____

15. customary   _____

B. *On the line provided, write a **verb** related to each of the following words.*

EXAMPLE: interrogation — **interrogate**

1. animated   _____

2. poised   _____

3. available   _____

4. oration   _____

5. indispensable   _____

6. customary   _____

7. peevish   _____

8. interminable   _____

Filling the Blanks

Encircle the pair of words or expressions that best complete each of the following passages.

1. Running our country is full of all kinds of hidden _____ and traps for the unwary. For that reason, no President, no matter how alert or cautious he may be, ever leaves office entirely _____ by the experience.

   a. regimes . . . lubricated
   b. firebrands . . . poised
   c. ingredients . . . animated
   d. hazards . . . unscathed

2. When I was very young, I truly _____ a life of excitement, adventure, and danger. But now that I'm a good deal older, I'm perfectly content with my rather _____ existence.

   a. brooded about . . . interminable
   b. yearned for . . . humdrum
   c. alighted on . . . trivial
   d. indulged in . . . hazardous

3. Though crabmeat is one of the _____ mentioned in the classic recipe for a New Orleans fish stew, it isn't always "in season." Accordingly, professional chefs often replace it with whatever shellfish is _____ at the time without any noticeable damage to the dish.

   a. résumés . . . adjacent
   b. broods . . . indispensable
   c. ingredients . . . available
   d. orations . . . customary

4. At one point in last night's hockey game, home-team fans became so angry with the referee that they began to _____ him with refuse. Programs, paper cups, and even a dead fish _____ through the air and landed at his feet.

   a. pelt . . . hurtled
   b. disrupt . . . droned
   c. indulge . . . loomed
   d. singe . . . trickled

5. Strong winds fanned the flames, and the fire in the factory quickly spread to _____ buildings. Though the fire fighters worked very hard to _____ its progress, the blaze soon engulfed the entire block.

   a. available . . . goad
   b. adjacent . . . retard
   c. miscellaneous . . . animate
   d. upright . . . germinate

6. When the new _____ took office, its first order of business was to pacify the country by arranging a permanent _____ with the rebel forces that had been waging all-out war against the previous administration.

   a. dynasty . . . plague
   b. drone . . . homicide
   c. firebrand . . . loom
   d. regime . . . truce

Unit 4

Definitions

Note carefully the spelling, pronunciation, and definition of each of the following words. Then write the word in the blank space in the illustrative phrase following.

1. **alliance**
   (ə 'lī əns)

   (*n.*) a joining together for some common purpose

   a wartime _____

2. **bewilder**
   (bi 'wil dər)

   (*v.*) to puzzle completely, confuse

   _____ by their behavior

3. **buffoon**
   (bə 'fün)

   (*n.*) a clown; a coarse, stupid person

   play the _____

4. **controversial**
   (kän trə 'vər shəl)

   (*adj.*) arousing argument, dispute, or disagreement

   a _____ proposal

5. **dishearten**
   (dis 'härt ən)

   (*v.*) to discourage

   _____ by the poor results

6. **fruitless**
   ('früt ləs)

   (*adj.*) not producing the desired results, unsuccessful

   when their efforts proved _____

7. **hostile**
   ('häs təl)

   (*adj.*) unfriendly; unfavorable; warlike, aggressive

   a _____ attitude

8. **inflammable**
   (in 'flam ə bəl)

   (*adj.*) easily set on fire; easily angered or aroused

   a highly _____ material

9. **inflict**
   (in 'flikt)

   (*v.*) to give or cause something unpleasant, impose

   _____ pain on others

10. **malignant**
    (mə 'lig nənt)

    (*adj.*) deadly, extremely harmful, evil; spiteful, malicious

    a _____ growth

11. **mortify**
    ('môrt ə fī)

    (*v.*) to hurt someone's feelings deeply; to cause embarrassment or humiliation; to subdue or discipline by self-denial or suffering

    _____ by their behavior

12. **orthodox**
    ('ôr thə däks)

    (*adj.*) in agreement with established or generally accepted beliefs or ways of doing things

    an _____ belief

13. **procure**
    (prə 'kyür)

    (*v.*) to obtain through special effort; to bring about

    _____ the necessary funds

14. **scurry**
    ('skər ē)

    (*v.*) to run quickly, scamper, hurry

    _____ back to their seats

15. **sodden**
    ('säd ən)

    (*adj.*) soaked with liquid or moisture; expressionless, dull; spiritless, listless

    _____ marshlands

16. spirited
('spir ə tid)

(*adj.*) full of life and vigor; courageous

a _____ defense

17. virtual
('vər chü əl)

(*adj.*) having a certain force or effect in fact but not in name; so close as to be equivalent to the real thing

a _____ dictator

18. void
(void)

(*adj.*) completely empty; having no legal force or effect; (*n.*) empty or unfilled space; (*v.*) to cancel or nullify

left a great _____ in my life

19. wayward
('wā wərd)

(*adj.*) disobedient, willful; unpredictable, capricious

the _____ path of a comet

20. wince
(wins)

(*v.*) to draw back suddenly, as though in pain or fear; (*n.*) the act of drawing back in this way

_____ in pain

Completing the Sentence

Choose the word from this unit that best completes each of the following sentences. Write the word in the space provided.

1. Even though I'm an adult, I still _____ in discomfort at the thought of a trip to the dentist.

2. Though the gallant defenders of the Alamo were hopelessly outnumbered, they put up a truly _____ fight.

3. Despite the fact that she has no official title of any kind, she has become the _____ director of the company.

4. When the naughty children heard their mother's footsteps approaching, they quickly _____ back to bed.

5. I was thoroughly _____ when I suddenly stumbled and spilled punch all over the hostess's new gown.

6. The frozen wastes of the Arctic may seem _____ to human life, but in fact thousands of Eskimos are able to survive there.

7. If it is allowed to spread unchecked, the poison of racial prejudice will have a decidedly _____ effect on our community.

8. The court of many a medieval king or prince was enlivened by the pranks and antics of jesters and other _____ .

9. Their behavior is so _____ and unpredictable that I never know what they are going to do next.

10. The directions he gave us for driving to the beach were so complicated that I was completely _____ by them.

11. Before we set out on the camping trip, I was given sole responsibility for

_____ all the necessary equipment and supplies.

12. Some parts of the President's proposal were agreeable to everyone; others

proved highly _____ .

13. In 1949, the United States formed a(n) _____ with eleven

other nations, organized into the North Atlantic Treaty Organization.

14. We _____ such heavy casualties on the enemy that they

were forced to break off the engagement and retreat.

15. After four days of steady rainfall, the _____ ground actually

gurgled as we trudged wearily over it.

16. Since the gas did not burn when we brought a flame to it, the experiment

showed that carbon dioxide is not _____ .

17. When the Supreme Court finds a law unconstitutional, that law is said to be

null and _____ .

18. Even though you like to do things in your own way, I suggest that you first

learn the _____ method of batting.

19. Would it be a bad pun if I were to say that our attempts to set up an apple

orchard have proved to be _____ ?

20. Refusing to be _____ by her early failures to find a summer

job, Lucy made up her mind to try again.

Synonyms *Choose the word from this unit that is most nearly **the same** in meaning as each of the following groups of expressions. Write the word on the line given.*

1. to flinch, shudder, recoil _____

2. disobedient, perverse; unpredictable _____

3. to rush, dash, scamper, scramble _____

4. lively, animated; courageous, gallant _____

5. useless, vain, unproductive, futile _____

6. warlike, aggressive; unfriendly _____

7. invalid; empty, vacant, bare; to cancel _____

8. to confuse, baffle, perplex _____

9. drenched, waterlogged, saturated _____

10. to humiliate, embarrass, abash _____

11. combustible, easily ignited; excitable _____

12. to discourage, dismay

13. functioning as, equivalent to

14. deadly, lethal; wicked, malicious

15. a pact, league, coalition

16. to obtain, gain, acquire; to achieve

17. a jester, clown, "wise guy"

18. to deal out, visit upon, impose

19. disputed, arguable, debatable

20. traditional, standard, customary

Antonyms *Choose the word from this unit that is most nearly opposite in meaning to each of the following groups of expressions. Write the word on the line given.*

1. to encourage, raise one's spirits

2. fireproof, fire-resistant; calm

3. to trudge, plod, creep, crawl

4. lifeless, dull, lackluster

5. docile, well-behaved; predictable

6. parched, arid, dry as a bone

7. wholesome, beneficial, benign

8. productive, effective, having results

9. unusual, unconventional, heretical

10. in effect; teeming with; to confirm

11. not likely to cause a fuss

12. not to bat an eyelid at

13. to set straight, enlighten

14. friendly, cordial; peaceful

15. someone who is serious and dignified

16. to fail to obtain, come away empty-handed

17. a parting of the ways, rift, split

18. to suffer, undergo, sustain

4

Choosing the Right Word *Encircle the **boldface** word that more satisfactorily completes each of the following sentences.*

1. Because I no longer go to high school, my student bus pass has been (**voided, disheartened**).

2. Mr. Hall, our supervisor, gives the impression of being an easygoing man, but we have learned that he has a very (**orthodox, inflammable**) temper.

3. Being scolded for my shortcomings in front of the entire basketball squad was a truly (**mortifying, wayward**) experience for me.

4. "Whenever you find (**wayward, controversial**) children," the speaker said, "you also find ineffective parents."

5. Walking through the meadow at night, we could hear mice and other small animals (**scurrying, wincing**) about in the grass.

6. The scrappy coach's (**fruitless, spirited**) pep talk lifted the team out of its "losing-season blues" almost overnight.

7. I still (**scurry, wince**) when I think of the two bad errors that cost us the championship game.

8. In high school, young people should (**procure, void**) training in basic skills that they will need to qualify for good jobs in later life.

9. A severe cold spell in December (**inflicted, bewildered**) heavy losses on the Florida citrus crop.

10. "It's hard not to be a little (**procured, disheartened**) when your favorite team is in the cellar two weeks before the playoffs," I replied.

11. Instead of being so (**mortified, hostile**), why don't you try to show some friendliness to those newcomers?

12. I can understand that you want to be witty and amusing, but take care not to give everyone the impression that you're a mere (**alliance, buffoon**).

13. When his army seemed (**virtually, soddenly**) defeated by the British, George Washington crossed the Delaware and won a major victory.

14. I could see from the (**inflicted, bewildered**) expression on the child's face that he was quite lost.

15. Though her views about the role of women in society are far from (**hostile, orthodox**), even conservatives and traditionalists listen to them.

16. Any (**fruitless, controversial**) political figure is likely to have as many critics as he or she has supporters.

17. (**Malignant, Virtual**) gossip has unjustly damaged their reputation.

18. We are going to form a broad (**void, alliance**) among all the groups that are working to improve life in our community.

19. On the hottest night of the whole summer, the sheets on my bed became so (**sodden, malignant**) with perspiration that I had to change them.

20. All our efforts to control pollution will be (**fruitless, inflammable**) unless we work out a careful, detailed plan in advance.

Unit 5

Definitions

Note carefully the spelling, pronunciation, and definition of each of the following words. Then write the word in the blank space in the illustrative phrase following.

1. anecdote
('an ek dōt)

(*n.*) a short account of an incident in someone's life

told a humorous _____

2. consolidate
(kən 'säl ə dāt)

(*v.*) to combine, unite; to make solid or firm

_____ our forces

3. counterfeit
('kaùn tər fit)

(*n.*) an imitation designed to deceive; (*adj.*) not genuine, fake; (*v.*) to make an illegal copy

_____ stamps

4. docile
('däs əl)

(*adj.*) easily taught, led, or managed; obedient

_____ children

5. dominate
('däm ə nāt)

(*v.*) to rule over by strength or power, control; to tower over, command due to height

_____ the meeting

6. entreat
(en 'trēt)

(*v.*) to beg, implore, ask earnestly

_____ them for help

7. fallible
('fal ə bəl)

(*adj.*) capable of being wrong, mistaken, or inaccurate

_____ methods

8. fickle
('fik əl)

(*adj.*) liable to change very rapidly, erratic; marked by a lack of constancy or steadiness, inconsistent

a truly _____ person

9. fugitive
('fyü jə tiv)

(*n.*) one who flees or runs away; (*adj.*) fleeting, lasting a very short time; wandering; difficult to grasp

a _____ from justice

10. grimy
('grī mē)

(*adj.*) very dirty, covered with dirt or soot

the _____ faces of the miners

11. iota
(ī 'ō tə)

(*n.*) a very small part or quantity

without an _____ of evidence

12. maul
(môl)

(*v.*) to beat or knock about, handle roughly; to mangle; (*n.*) a heavy hammer

_____ by the lion

13. potential
(pə 'ten chəl)

(*adj.*) possible, able to happen; (*n.*) something that can develop or become a reality

a _____ threat

14. radiant
('rā dē ənt)

(*adj.*) shining, bright; giving forth light or energy

a _____ smile

5

15. rural
('rür əl)

(*adj.*) relating to farm areas and life in the country

a _____ community

16. substantial
(səb 'stan shəl)

(*adj.*) large, important; major, significant; prosperous; not imaginary, material

a _____ raise in salary

17. tactful
('takt fəl)

(*adj.*) skilled in handling difficult situations or people, polite

a _____ remark

18. tamper
('tam pər)

(*v.*) to interfere with; to meddle rashly or foolishly with; to handle in a secret and improper way

_____ with the baggage

19. ultimate
('əl tə mət)

(*adj.*) last, final; most important or extreme; eventual; basic, fundamental

our _____ destiny

20. uncertainty
(ən 'sər tən tē)

(*n.*) doubt, the state of being unsure

_____ about the future

Completing the Sentence

Choose the word from this unit that best completes each of the following sentences. Write it in the space given.

1. Though the UN has many lesser objectives, its _____ goal is to achieve lasting world peace.

2. After living so long in a large city, I was happy to spend a few weeks in those beautiful _____ surroundings.

3. The boat has been so badly _____ by the storm that it will have to be overhauled before it can be used again.

4. Unwilling to bear the _____ any longer, I called the Dean of Admissions to find out if I had been accepted.

5. To be _____ in everyday life means doing whatever you can to avoid hurting the feelings of other people.

6. We discovered that there was not a(n) _____ of truth in the rumors that they had spread so eagerly.

7. Since I had expected the children to be hard to handle, I was pleasantly surprised by their _____ behavior.

8. I took my broken TV set to a qualified repair service, rather than run the risk of damaging it further by _____ with it myself.

9. The Board of Education believes it would save considerable money to _____ three small schools into one big school.

10. As she told us the good news, her face was _____ with joy.

11. The new book of Presidential _____ contains many amusing stories involving our Chief Executives, both past and present.

12. There is an old saying that pencils are made with erasers because human beings are _____ .

13. Trying desperately to avoid the police, the _____ hid in the cellar of the abandoned house.

14. "As a mother," Mrs. Roerich said to the judge, "I _____ you to show leniency toward my son."

15. The taste of the public is so _____ that a TV performer who is a big hit one season may be out of a job the next.

16. Since all of our cashiers handle large sums of money, we have given them special training in recognizing _____ bills.

17. Despite the doctor's best efforts, there has been no _____ change in the patient's condition for weeks.

18. The windows had become so _____ and spotted that it took me some time to get them clean.

19. The wily old Senator had such a forceful and aggressive personality that he soon came to _____ his entire party.

20. Though Company A has very little chance of expanding in the near future, the _____ growth rate of Company B is staggering.

Synonyms   *Choose the word from this unit that is most nearly* **the same** *in meaning as each of the following groups of expressions. Write the word on the line given.*

1. glowing, brilliant, dazzling, resplendent   _____

2. farthest, furthest; final, terminal   _____

3. a possibility, capability; possible   _____

4. to meddle with, monkey with, fool with   _____

5. significant, considerable; tangible   _____

6. to rough up, manhandle; to mangle   _____

7. filthy, sooty, soiled, dirt-encrusted   _____

8. skillful; diplomatic, discreet   _____

9. a speck, dab, jot, bit, smidgen   _____

10. inconsistent, erratic; capricious   _____

11. imperfect, open to error _____

12. false, fake, phony, bogus _____

13. to control, gain the upper hand _____

14. to strengthen, firm up; to combine, merge _____

15. to plead, beg, implore, beseech _____

16. obedient, manageable, teachable _____

17. doubtfulness, unsureness; hesitation _____

18. a runaway, deserter; elusive _____

19. a tale, story, sketch, vignette, yarn _____

20. countrified, rustic _____

Antonyms   *Choose the word from this unit that is most nearly* **opposite** *in meaning to each of the following groups of expressions. Write the word on the line given.*

1. genuine, real, authentic, not fake _____

2. spotless, spick-and-span, immaculate _____

3. to handle with kid gloves _____

4. lasting, enduring, permanent _____

5. actual, real; unlikely, impossible _____

6. a flood, deluge, avalanche, glut _____

7. unruly, wayward, intractable, disobedient _____

8. constant, steady, invariable _____

9. minor, insignificant, negligible _____

10. first, initial; most immediate, nearest _____

11. urban, metropolitan, citified _____

12. to be under someone's thumb _____

13. to scatter, disperse, dissipate, separate _____

14. foolproof, unfailing, flawless _____

15. dull, tarnished, lackluster _____

16. clumsy, gauche, boorish, indiscreet _____

17. sureness, certainty; confidence _____

18. to demand forcefully, clamor for _____

Choosing the Right Word *Encircle the **boldface** word that more satisfactorily completes each of the following sentences.*

1. Evidence showed that the lawyer had tried to (**consolidate, tamper**) with the witnesses by offering them bribes to change their testimony.

2. Throughout the course of its history, the United States has opened its gates to (**fugitives, counterfeits**) from tyranny in other lands.

3. The only certain thing in life is that there will always be many (**fugitives, uncertainties**).

4. I suspected that his expression of happiness was (**potential, counterfeit**) and that he was really jealous of our success.

5. Although the ideals of my youth have been (**entreated, mauled**) by hard experience, they have not been totally destroyed.

6. It wasn't very (**docile, tactful**) of you to tell her that she seemed to have gained weight.

7. Larry got good grades on the midterm tests, but he is headed for trouble because he hasn't done an (**anecdote, iota**) of work since then.

8. The Mayor has no chance for reelection unless she can (**consolidate, maul**) the different groups and forces supporting her.

9. Imagine someone as changeable as George having the nerve to say that I'm (**radiant, fickle**)!

10. In modern hospitals, everything possible is done to prevent and control mistakes resulting from human (**fallibility, fickleness**).

11. I found his (**anecdotes, entreaties**) amusing, but I fail to see what they had to do with the central ideas of his talk.

12. If you want to see the (**iota, ultimate**) in shoe styles, ask Beth to show you the new sandals she bought for the spring dance.

13. The young man who seemed so quiet and (**docile, substantial**) turned out to be very well informed and to have strong opinions of his own.

14. As soon as 300-pound Horace settled down in that delicate little chair, we realized he should have something more (**grimy, substantial**) to sit on.

15. The (**ultimate, rural**) population of the United States is growing smaller, but the people living on farms are as important as ever to the nation.

16. How can we properly direct the (**uncertainties, potential**) for good and evil in each of us into useful channels?

17. There, in the very heart of the noisy and (**grimy, fallible**) city, was a truly beautiful little park with green lawns, flowers, and a fountain.

18. Rarely in our history has a single man so (**dominated, entreated**) the Federal government as Franklin D. Roosevelt did during the 1930's.

19. One of our best hopes of solving the energy problem lies in making direct use of (**radiant, fugitive**) energy from the sun.

20. I know from personal experience how much harm smoking can do, and I (**dominate, entreat**) you not to get started on that miserable habit.

Unit 6

Definitions

Note carefully the spelling, pronunciation, and definition of each of the following words. Then write the word in the blank space in the illustrative phrase following.

1. anonymous
(ə 'nän ə məs)

(*adj.*) unnamed, without the name of the person involved (writer, composer, etc.); unknown; lacking individuality or character

an _____ tip

2. browse
(braüz)

(*v.*) to nibble, graze; to read casually; to window-shop

_____ through a book

3. dupe
(düp)

(*n.*) a person easily tricked or deceived; (*v.*) to deceive

_____ into betraying his trust

4. dynamic
(dī 'nam ik)

(*adj.*) active, energetic, forceful

a _____ personality

5. eradicate
(i 'rad ə kāt)

(*v.*) to root out, get rid of, destroy completely

_____ a disease

6. frustrate
('frəs trāt)

(*v.*) to prevent from accomplishing a purpose or fulfilling a desire; to cause feelings of discouragement

_____ our plan

7. grim
(grim)

(*adj.*) stern, merciless; fierce, savage, cruel

the _____ prospect of famine

8. inimitable
(in 'im ə tə bəl)

(*adj.*) not capable of being copied or imitated

her _____ smile

9. makeshift
('māk shift)

(*n.*) a temporary substitute for something else; (*adj.*) crude, flimsy, or temporary

_____ sleeping quarters

10. marginal
('märj ə nəl)

(*adj.*) in, at, or near the edge or margin; only barely good, large, or important enough for the purpose

_____ farmland

11. pending
('pen diŋ)

(*adj.*) waiting to be settled; (*prep.*) until

_____ the judge's decision

12. prescribe
(pri 'skrīb)

(*v.*) to order as a rule or course to be followed; to order for medical purposes

_____ complete rest

13. preview
('prē vyü)

(*n.*) something seen in advance; (*v.*) to view beforehand

a _____ of the new movie

14. prominent
('präm ə nənt)

(*adj.*) standing out so as to be easily seen; important, well-known

a _____ figure in society

15. quaint
(kwānt)

(*adj.*) odd or old-fashioned in a pleasing way; clever, ingenious; skillfully made

_____ customs

16. reluctant
(ri 'lək tənt)

(*adj.*) unwilling, holding back

a _____ witness

17. scrimp
(skrimp)

(*v.*) to handle very economically or stingily; to supply in a way that is small, short, or scanty

forced to _____ and save

18. snare
(snâr)

(*v.*) to trap, catch; (*n.*) a trap or entanglement

caught in a _____

19. utmost
('ət mōst)

(*adj.*) greatest, highest, furthest; (*n.*) the extreme limit

tried her _____ to learn Greek

20. vengeance
('ven jəns)

(*n.*) punishment in return for an injury or a wrong; unusual force or violence

took _____ on their enemies

Completing the Sentence

Choose the word from this unit that best completes each of the following sentences. Write the word in the space provided.

1. For weeks I _____ on everything to save enough money to buy the replacement tires for my bicycle.

2. The most _____ feature of the skyline of that little town in Iowa is the four-story grain elevator.

3. Many books have been written about boys, but none of them can match the _____ qualities of *Tom Sawyer* and *Huckleberry Finn*.

4. Instead of seeking personal _____ for the wrong that has been done to you, why don't you look for justice under the law?

5. When we visited Salem, Massachusetts, last year, we were charmed by the _____ 18th-century houses in the town.

6. There is quite a contrast between the _____ administration that now runs that country and the "do-nothing" regime that preceded it.

7. Safety measures are of the _____ importance when you are planning a canoe trip over rivers filled with dangerous rapids.

8. Each unit in the textbook opens with a section that _____ and highlights the material in the chapters that follow.

9. When unexpected guests turned up on the doorstep, I hurriedly made a few _____ arrangements to accommodate them.

10. The suspect was held in the local police station _____ the outcome of the investigation.

11. I was _____ into trusting him, and I have paid a heavy price for being misled so easily.

12. After the fisherman _____ the fish, he unhooked it from his line and threw it back into the stream.

13. It took the druggist about an hour to prepare the medicine that the doctor had _____ for my cold.

14. After several unsuccessful attempts to catch the waiter's eye, I began to become a little _____ .

15. Although we know who wrote such famous epics as the *Aeneid* and the *Iliad*, the author of *Beowulf* remains _____ .

16. Ellen was _____ to tell the police all that she had seen, but we convinced her that it was the only right thing to do.

17. We may not be able to _____ crime in our community, but if we go about it in the right way, I am sure we can reduce it greatly.

18. Is there any sight in the world more restful than cows _____ in a meadow alongside a little brook?

19. I like to write _____ notes in a book alongside important material, but I never do so unless the book belongs to me.

20. When we saw the _____ expression on the poor man's face, we realized that the situation was indeed serious.

Synonyms   *Choose the word from this unit that is most nearly **the same** in meaning as each of the following groups of expressions. Write the word on the line given.*

1. picturesque; peculiar, strange, curious   _____

2. matchless, incomparable, unique   _____

3. an advance showing; a foretaste   _____

4. stern; dreadful, frightful; ferocious   _____

5. to destroy, wipe out, root out   _____

6. standing out, conspicuous, noticeable   _____

7. borderline, minimal, peripheral   _____

8. undecided, unsettled, awaiting action   _____

9. to economize, pinch pennies, cut corners   _____

10. a trap, pitfall; to trap, catch   _____

11. to order, specify, appoint, recommend   _____

12. energetic, vigorous, high-powered   _____

13. revenge, retaliation, reprisal   _____

14. to skim, scan, dip into; to graze   _____

15. to thwart, foil, baffle; to disappoint   _____

16. hesitant, unwilling, loath, disinclined   _____

17. temporary, stopgap; substitute; flimsy   _____

18. nameless, unknown   _____

19. highest, maximum, greatest, supreme, best   _____

20. to fool, mislead, hoodwink, delude   _____

Antonyms   _Choose the word from this unit that is most nearly_ **opposite** _in meaning to each of the following groups of expressions. Write the word on the line given._

1. to splurge, throw money around   _____

2. willing, eager, inclined   _____

3. settled, decided, resolved   _____

4. to implant, instill; to foster, promote   _____

5. inconspicuous, unnoticeable, obscure   _____

6. to help, assist, abet   _____

7. familiar, commonplace; modern, contemporary   _____

8. mild; merciful; delightful   _____

9. central, pivotal, focal   _____

10. to set straight, undeceive, disabuse   _____

11. least, smallest possible   _____

12. permanent, durable; solid, sturdy   _____

13. lazy, lackadaisical, lethargic, sluggish   _____

14. able to be copied or reproduced   _____

15. forgiveness, pardon, turning the other cheek   _____

16. to pore over, study carefully, scrutinize   _____

17. with a known or identifiable author   _____

18. to set free, let loose, liberate   _____

Choosing the Right Word   *Encircle the **boldface** word that more satisfactorily completes each of the following sentences.*

1. He still doesn't realize that he has been used as a (**dupe, scrimp**) by our opponents to do their dirty work for them.

2. The new parking regulations are only a (**snare, makeshift**) that will have to be replaced by a better plan within a few years.

3. Even before we saw Alice, we heard her (**inimitable, grim**) high-pitched giggle and knew she was at the party.

4. It is very easy to say that our city government should (**scrimp, snare**) to balance its budget, but which departments should spend less?

5. We have many good musicians in our school orchestra, but they need a (**makeshift, dynamic**) conductor to make them play as a unit.

6. For months the winter was unusually mild, but when the cold weather did come, it struck with a (**vengeance, prominence**).

7. You must realize that, although we may find the customs of other lands (**anonymous, quaint**), they are just part of everyday life in those areas.

8. Although the announcement had promised us "a (**prominent, reluctant**) speaker," the person turned out to be a very minor public official.

9. Landing a man on the moon was a great achievement, but it is far from being the (**utmost, pending**) limit of our space program.

10. Since my job is only (**marginal, inimitable**), I'm afraid that if business falls off a little, they may let me go.

11. (**Pending, Eradicating**) the outcome of our national election, none of the foreign governments is willing to take any definite action.

12. His reference to a "historical downfall" after I had failed the history test struck me as a rather (**dynamic, grim**) joke.

13. As I was (**previewing, browsing**) my way lazily through the newspaper, I was shocked to see my own name in a headline!

14. The mistaken idea that the most important thing in life is to "have fun" is a (**snare, vengeance**) that leads to serious trouble for many young people.

15. Nothing can (**eradicate, scrimp**) the love of liberty from the hearts of a free people!

16. Although we cannot mention her by name, we want to express our heartfelt gratitude to the (**quaint, anonymous**) donor who gave us this generous gift.

17. The exhibition at the fair is intended to give people a (**preview, dupe**) of what life may be like fifty years from now.

18. I understand your (**reluctance, vengeance**) to be our candidate in the next election, but I think it is your duty to accept the nomination.

19. To improve your unsatisfactory school record, I would (**browse, prescribe**) regular doses of study, to be taken every day for as long as is necessary.

20. The wily champion used every tennis trick she knew to (**frustrate, scrimp**) her opponent's attempts to come to the net and hit a winner.

Review Units 4–6

Analogies   *In each of the following, encircle the item that best completes the comparison.*

1. dynamic is to **energy** as
a. fickle is to courage
b. malignant is to benefit
c. spirited is to vigor
d. makeshift is to substance

2. procure is to **obtain** as
a. consolidate is to disperse
b. inflict is to observe
c. eradicate is to implant
d. snare is to trap

3. scurry is to **fast** as
a. maul is to slow
b. tamper is to fast
c. browse is to slow
d. dominate is to fast

4. barn is to **rural** as
a. skyscraper is to urban
b. subway is to rural
c. corral is to urban
d. tenement is to rural

5. fruitless is to **result** as
a. heartless is to skill
b. aimless is to direction
c. tactless is to merit
d. priceless is to value

6. blunder is to **mortify** as
a. victory is to frustrate
b. agreement is to bewilder
c. pleasure is to wince
d. defeat is to dishearten

7. inimitable is to **copy** as
a. unpredictable is to foresee
b. uncomfortable is to wear
c. undesirable is to enjoy
d. undeniable is to prove

8. wayward is to **docile** as
a. ultimate is to final
b. void is to empty
c. hostile is to friendly
d. quaint is to charming

9. con artist is to **dupe** as
a. patient is to prescribe
b. buffoon is to amuse
c. fugitive is to reward
d. ally is to dominate

10. anecdote is to **incident** as
a. lyric is to emotion
b. opera is to ambition
c. drama is to opinion
d. epic is to concern

11. fugitive is to **flee** as
a. buffoon is to browse
b. lawyer is to scrimp
c. beggar is to entreat
d. doctor is to wince

12. substantial is to **much** as
a. marginal is to little
b. pending is to much
c. utmost is to little
d. void is to much

13. alliance is to **agree** as
a. preview is to disagree
b. anecdote is to agree
c. controversy is to disagree
d. vengeance is to agree

14. fallible is to **err** as
a. anonymous is to discover
b. wayward is to obey
c. dynamic is to delay
d. fickle is to change

15. mountain is to **prominent** as
a. valley is to virtual
b. marsh is to sodden
c. orchard is to potential
d. desert is to makeshift

16. racehorse is to **spirited** as
a. pony is to malignant
b. mule is to reluctant
c. donkey is to controversial
d. colt is to tactful

17. puzzle is to **bewilder** as
a. iota is to delight
b. anecdote is to dishearten
c. uncertainty is to comfort
d. stalemate is to frustrate

18. sheen is to **radiant** as
a. blemish is to splendid
b. tarnish is to dull
c. luster is to grimy
d. glow is to inflammable

Identification *In each of the following groups, encircle the word that is best defined or suggested by the introductory phrase.*

1. taking pains not to hurt someone's feelings
a. wayward   b. tactful   c. reluctant   d. virtual

2. "Have you heard the story about _____?"
a. grim   b. makeshift   c. anecdote   d. controversial

3. something that the doctor does
a. prescribe   b. preview   c. bewilder   d. wince

4. "I haven't got a clue."
a. inflict   b. dominate   c. preview   d. bewilder

5. like a sheep
a. fallible   b. docile   c. dynamic   d. reluctant

6. find the equipment we need for the trip
a. procure   b. mortify   c. scurry   d. dominate

7. to pull something out by the roots
a. browse   b. scrimp   c. entreat   d. eradicate

8. "Ouch!"
a. wince   b. tamper   c. void   d. dupe

9. stray from the straight and narrow
a. rural   b. marginal   c. wayward   d. orthodox

10. "I'm afraid that I won't be able to find a job this summer."
a. substantial   b. malignant   c. grimy   d. disheartened

11. The North Atlantic Treaty Organization (NATO)
a. iota   b. snare   c. alliance   d. uncertainty

12. given to sudden and unexpected changes of mood
a. fickle   b. docile   c. dynamic   d. potential

13. a court jester
a. prominent   b. vengeance   c. pending   d. buffoon

14. rather badly chewed up by a tiger
a. consolidate   b. maul   c. frustrate   d. inflammable

15. not at all foolproof
a. inflict   b. inimitable   c. fallible   d. utmost

16. a whole lot of nothing
a. void   b. anecdote   c. vengeance   d. snare

Shades of Meaning *Read each sentence carefully. Then encircle the item that best completes the statement below the sentence.*

The suburban building boom of the 1950s saw entire developments of anonymous tract houses spring up practically overnight. (2)

1. The word **anonymous** in line 2 most nearly means
a. nameless   c. unknown
b. indistinguishable   d. inexpensive

With three straight primary victories the candidate consolidated her
position as front-runner for the nomination of her party. **(2)**

2. The best definition for **consolidated** in line 1 is
a. strengthened   b. united   c. merged   d. combined

In some early religious orders, members mortified their bodies by fasting
and even, in some cases, by voluntarily suffering physical pain. **(2)**

3. In line 1 the word **mortified** is best defined as
a. embarrassed   b. disciplined   c. humiliated   d. strengthened

Perhaps the hectic touring schedule had taken its toll on the cast; at any
rate I found last night's performance of the play decidedly sodden. **(2)**

4. The word **sodden** in line 2 is used to mean
a. drenched   b. brilliant   c. listless   d. soaked

Physicists use huge devices called particle accelerators to explore the
ultimate building blocks of matter. **(2)**

5. In line 2 the word **ultimate** most nearly means
a. basic   c. eventual
b. final   d. most important

Antonyms   *In each of the following groups, encircle the word or
expression that is most nearly **opposite** in meaning to
the **boldface word** in the introductory phrase.*

1. the **uncertainty** of the situation
a. doubtfulness   b. newness   c. strangeness   d. sureness

2. a **rural** community
a. urban   b. foreign   c. sizable   d. new

3. **orthodox** beliefs
a. familiar   b. heretical   c. interesting   d. puzzling

4. a **malignant** growth
a. harmless   b. dangerous   c. ugly   d. unexplained

5. a **grim** look
a. happy   b. sad   c. horrified   d. stern

6. a **prominent** attorney
a. wealthy   b. unselfish   c. famous   d. obscure

7. played a **marginal** part in the victory
a. central   b. laughable   c. secondary   d. unworthy

8. a **fruitless** attempt
a. successful   b. well-planned   c. exhausting   d. failing

9. made me a **substantial** loan
a. large   b. small   c. generous   d. personal

10. **makeshift** arrangements
a. temporary   b. durable   c. worthless   d. complicated

R

11. a **spirited** reply
a. amusing b. lackluster c. bitter d. firm

12. an **iota** of common sense
a. glut b. result c. smidgen d. failure

13. **snare** the animal
a. capture b. kill c. release d. feed

14. **scurry** off to bed
a. scamper b. fly c. run d. trudge

15. a **potential** threat to the environment
a. possible b. real c. new d. minor

Completing the Sentence *From the following words, choose the one that best completes each of the sentences below. Write the word in the space provided.*

Group A

hostile	entreat	scrimp	dominate
rural	dishearten	quaint	inflict
grim	pending	radiant	sodden

1. The speaker said that in any future war between major powers, each will be in a position to _____ terrible damage on the other.

2. We have solved some problems, but those still _____ will require our full attention.

3. It is true that she is very well informed, but that is no excuse for her rudeness in trying to _____ the conversation.

4. In this great emergency, we _____ everyone who can donate blood to report to the hospital immediately.

5. Since I am used to city life, I usually become restless after spending a few days in a(n) _____ setting.

Group B

wince	controversial	procure	spirited
alliance	bewilder	tamper	maul
utmost	makeshift	uncertainty	anecdote

1. To deal effectively with our pressing pollution problems, we must have a(n) _____ among government, business, and consumers.

2. I feel a sense of _____ about whether or not I should prepare to study engineering.

3. This particular bill is so _____ that trying to get the state legislature to pass it is not going to be an easy matter.

4. Since the mechanic was not familiar with the diesel type of engine in our truck, he wisely refused to _____ with it.

5. If you try to explain too much in too short a time, all that you will do is to _____ the new employees.

Word Families

A. *On the line provided, write a **noun form** of each of the following words.*

EXAMPLE: reluctant — **reluctance**

1. entreat _____
2. hostile _____
3. orthodox _____
4. malignant _____
5. bewilder _____
6. prescribe _____
7. tactful _____
8. wayward _____
9. consolidate _____
10. quaint _____
11. controversial _____
12. mortify _____
13. spirited _____
14. dominate _____
15. fallible _____
16. fickle _____
17. radiant _____
18. prominent _____
19. frustrate _____
20. dynamic _____

B. *On the line provided, write a **verb** related to each of the following words.*

EXAMPLE: grimy — **begrime**

1. alliance _____
2. radiant _____
3. inflammable _____
4. controversial _____
5. vengeance _____

Filling the Blanks

Encircle the pair of words or expressions that best complete each of the following passages.

1. "His methods are hardly what I'd call _____ , but they do get results," the sales manager remarked about her star salesman. "If he took a more traditional approach to his job, the company's profits might not be so _____ ."
   - a. dynamic . . . disheartening
   - b. quaint . . . marginal
   - c. orthodox . . . substantial
   - d. controversial . . . fruitless

2. "The President's new economic program has stirred up a good deal of _____ on Capitol Hill," the reporter observed. "Some of the members of Congress are clearly in favor of the plan; others are definitely _____ to it."
   - a. vengeance . . . anonymous
   - b. controversy . . . hostile
   - c. bewilderment . . . malignant
   - d. uncertainty . . . reluctant

3. The book is full of highly amusing stories involving many people who were _____ at the time. One of these witty little _____ tells how a famous actress once used garlic to discourage a flirtatious leading man.
   - a. utmost . . . previews
   - b. inimitable . . . iotas
   - c. dominant . . . snares
   - d. prominent . . . anecdotes

4. I know that an injection of novocaine doesn't normally _____ a great deal of pain. Still, the mere thought of the dentist's sharp needle is enough to make me _____ in imaginary discomfort.
   - a. inflict . . . wince
   - b. consolidate . . . scurry
   - c. eradicate . . . maul
   - d. procure . . . scrimp

5. Two convicts escaped from the state prison last week. The police managed to recapture one of the _____ in a matter of hours. But their efforts to catch the other have so far proved _____ .
   - a. buffoons . . . fallible
   - b. counterfeits . . . void
   - c. fugitives . . . fruitless
   - d. dupes . . . wayward

6. Despite setbacks that would have _____ a less determined person, she continued to do her _____ to become the top tennis player in the world. For, as she herself admitted, she knew that she wouldn't succeed unless she gave the task her "very best shot."
   - a. mortified . . . potential
   - b. entreated . . . ultimate
   - c. frustrated . . . virtual
   - d. disheartened . . . utmost

Analogies   *In each of the following, encircle the item that best completes the comparison.*

1. fruitless is to **barren** as
a. substantial is to trivial
b. grimy is to immaculate
c. adjacent is to distant
d. transparent is to clear

2. humdrum is to **stimulation** as
a. spirited is to energy
b. literate is to intelligence
c. grim is to charm
d. sullen is to anger

3. missile is to **pelt** as
a. feather is to maul
b. net is to snare
c. firebrand is to douse
d. hose is to singe

4. dissuade is to **stubborn** as
a. dishearten is to confident
b. retard is to slow
c. indulge is to selfish
d. dupe is to cautious

5. anecdote is to **biography** as
a. homicide is to forgery
b. epic is to lyric
c. alliance is to treaty
d. toast is to oration

6. bewilder is to **uncertain** as
a. irritate is to peevish
b. control is to wayward
c. procure is to reluctant
d. dominate is to hostile

7. inimitable is to **unique** as
a. makeshift is to potential
b. customary is to strange
c. interminable is to endless
d. miscellaneous is to indignant

8. poised is to **mortify** as
a. determined is to frustrate
b. certain is to verify
c. fallible is to recompense
d. controversial is to counterfeit

9. quaint is to **charm** as
a. marginal is to bulk
b. anonymous is to interest
c. malignant is to use
d. animated is to liveliness

10. lead is to **docile** as
a. separate is to mutual
b. preview is to orthodox
c. overlook is to prominent
d. dupe is to gullible

Shades of Meaning   *Read each sentence carefully. Then encircle the item that best completes the statement below the sentence.*

No matter how vivid and lifelike it may seem, "virtual reality" is no more substantial than a dream.   **(2)**

1. The word **substantial** in line 2 is best defined as
a. important   b. prosperous   c. tangible   d. affordable

The quaint machines that Leonardo da Vinci sketched in his notebooks show him to have been as accomplished an inventor as he was a painter.   **(2)**

2. In line 1 the word **quaint** most nearly means
a. old-fashioned   c. odd
b. picturesque   d. ingenious

Of all the notions that humankind has ever pondered, is there any so fugitive as time?   **(2)**

3. The word **fugitive** in line 2 is best defined as
a. wandering   b. elusive   c. fleeting   d. puzzling

When we open *Alice in Wonderland,* we leave behind the trivial world to
which we are accustomed and inhabit for a time the fantastical, topsy-turvy   (2)
universe of the author's imagination.

4. In line 1 the word **trivial** most nearly means
   a. minor   b. petty   c. ordinary   d. real

Alice's adventures in Wonderland begin when she chases after a white
rabbit, dressed in a waistcoat, that has come pelting by.   (2)

5. The phrase **pelting by** in line 2 is used to mean
   a. shedding its fur   c. nibbling
   b. throwing things   d. hurrying by

**Filling
the Blanks**
      *Encircle the pair of words that best complete the
meaning of each of the following passages.*

1. She used to be a very cheerful and confident young woman, but she has
been so _____ of late by ill health and financial worries that
she has lost a good deal of her _____ good humor and
optimism.
   a. disheartened . . . sullen   c. plagued . . . customary
   b. unscathed . . . virtual   d. frustrated . . . vicious

2. Gaius Julius Caesar's rivals in the Senate bitterly criticized the political
_____ he formed with Pompey and Crassus as a thinly
veiled attempt to overthrow the Republic and _____ the
Roman world by becoming its undisputed masters.
   a. dynasty . . . eradicate   c. regime . . . hurtle
   b. alliance . . . dominate   d. iota . . . disrupt

3. Just as a surgeon might remove a(n) _____ tumor from our
bodies, we must _____ the cancer of racial and religious
prejudice from our hearts and minds.
   a. fugitive . . . singe   c. indispensable . . . void
   b. wayward . . . germinate   d. malignant . . . eradicate

4. The _____ of Cicero's reputation as one of the foremost
public speakers of his day shines as bright today as it did on the day he
first delivered that famous _____ over 2000 years ago.
   a. luster . . . oration   c. radiance . . . ingredient
   b. uncertainty . . . anecdote   d. prominence . . . résumé

5. Eventually I _____ them from attempting to retaliate for the
wrong done to them by reminding them of a famous passage in the Bible,
in which God says, "_____ is mine; I will repay."
   a. animated . . . Truce   c. culminated . . . Homicide
   b. dissuaded . . . Vengeance   d. seethed . . . Recompense

Unit 7

Note carefully the spelling, pronunciation, and definition of each of the following words. Then write the word in the blank space in the illustrative phrase following.

1. amiss
(ə 'mis)

(*adj.*) faulty, imperfect, not as it should be; (*adv.*) in a mistaken or improper way, wrongly

when things have gone _____

2. brawl
(brôl)

(*n.*) a noisy quarrel or fight; (*v.*) to quarrel or fight noisily

a barroom _____

3. detest
(di 'test)

(*v.*) to hate, dislike very much, loathe

_____ spinach

4. domestic
(də 'mes tik)

(*adj.*) native to a country, not foreign; relating to the life or affairs of a household; (*n.*) a household servant

a pleasant _____ setting

5. flagrant
('flā grənt)

(*adj.*) extremely bad, glaring; scandalous, notorious

_____ disregard for the law

6. flaw
(flô)

(*n.*) a slight fault, defect, crack

a _____ in the plan

7. fledgling
('flej liŋ)

(*n.*) an inexperienced person, beginner; a young bird about to leave the nest; (*adj.*) inexperienced, budding

a _____ officer

8. fluster
('fləs tər)

(*v.*) to make or become confused, agitated, or nervous; (*n.*) a state of confusion or agitation

became _____ and tongue-tied

9. foremost
('fôr mōst)

(*adj.*) chief, most important, primary; (*adv.*) in the first place

_____ among my interests

10. momentum
(mō 'ment əm)

(*n.*) the force or speed with which something moves

began to gain _____

11. notable
('nōt ə bəl)

(*adj.*) striking, remarkable; (*n.*) a person who is well known, distinguished, or outstanding in some way

a _____ event in our lives

12. nurture
('nər chər)

(*v.*) to bring up, care for, train, nourish; (*n.*) rearing, training, upbringing

_____ the young

13. paradox
('par ə däks)

(*n.*) a self-contradictory statement that on closer examination proves true; a person or thing with seemingly contradictory qualities

a total _____ as a person

14. perjury
('pər jə rē)

(*n.*) the act of swearing to a lie

convicted of _____

15. presume
(pri 'züm)

(*v.*) to take for granted, assume or suppose; to dare, take upon oneself, take liberties

_____ on our hospitality

16. prior
('prī ər)

(*adj.*) earlier, former

a _____ appointment

17. proficient
(prə 'fish ənt)

(*adj.*) skilled, expert, or capable in any field or activity

a _____ cook

18. salvo
('sal vō)

(*n.*) a burst of gunfire or cannon shot, often as a tribute or salute; a sudden burst of anything; a spirited verbal attack

a _____ of laughter

19. vigilant
('vij ə lənt)

(*adj.*) wide-awake, alert, watchful

_____ guards

20. wrath
(rath)

(*n.*) intense anger

fear the _____ of God

Completing the Sentence

Choose the word from this unit that best completes each of the following sentences. Write the word in the space provided.

1. I wouldn't call such a(n) _____ and premeditated lie merely a "minor lapse of memory."

2. Like a(n) _____ eagle about to leave the nest for the first time, our son is preparing to spend his first summer away from home.

3. Though his career as a whole was not particularly distinguished, he did score one _____ success on Broadway a few years ago.

4. Her parents _____ her musical talents by hiring the finest teachers and taking her to hear the performances of great musicians.

5. We suspected that something was _____ when he did not return home from school at the usual time.

6. I must warn you again that if you fail to tell the truth, you may lay yourself open to a charge of _____ .

7. The biggest financier in the United States is the housewife who controls the _____ food budget.

8. At what point does a spinning top lose sufficient _____ to topple over?

9. Some people truly love the music of such modern composers as Arnold Schoenberg or Igor Stravinsky; others absolutely _____ it.

10. In most respects she is a fine person, but excessive stubbornness is the one important _____ in her character.

11. We must be _____ in recognizing the early signs of decay in our community and move quickly to improve conditions.

12. That terrible instruments of war should in fact prove useful as guardians of the peace is one of the _____ of modern life.

13. I have no way of knowing for sure why she left, but I _____ that she had a good reason for doing so.

14. When two players suddenly started to throw punches at each other during last night's game, an ugly bench-clearing _____ ensued.

15. It's a fact that some important battles of the American Revolution occurred _____ to the signing of the Declaration of Independence.

16. In the old days, wooden battleships saluted their victorious admiral by repeatedly firing _____ of cannon shot from their decks.

17. First and _____ among her many outstanding qualities is her ability to understand the points of view of other people.

18. How do you explain the fact that some students who do poorly in math are highly _____ in figuring out batting averages?

19. I well remember how often during my childhood I felt the full force of my parents' _____ when I had done something wrong.

20. The speaker went right on with his speech, in no way _____ or disturbed by the jeers and catcalls of a few rowdy hecklers.

Synonyms   *Choose the word from this unit that is most nearly **the same** in meaning as each of the following groups of expressions. Write the word on the line given.*

1. an imperfection, defect, fault, blemish   _____

2. rage, fury, ire, choler, indignation   _____

3. drive, thrust, force, impetus   _____

4. alert, watchful, attentive, on one's toes   _____

5. to agitate, rattle, disconcert   _____

6. household; native; tame; a servant   _____

7. earlier, previous, before, anterior   _____

7

8. to despise, loathe, abhor _____

9. a scuffle, donnybrook; to spar, lock horns _____

10. false witness, lying under oath _____

11. noteworthy, remarkable, impressive _____

12. competent, adept, able, skilled, expert _____

13. a beginner, novice, tyro, neophyte _____

14. chief, leading, principal, paramount _____

15. to suppose, surmise; to trespass, infringe _____

16. to raise, rear, bring up; to foster _____

17. a riddle, enigma, anomaly, absurdity _____

18. faulty, awry, not as it should be _____

19. a barrage, volley, burst _____

20. glaring, blatant, gross, outrageous _____

Antonyms   *Choose the word from this unit that is most nearly* **opposite** *in meaning to each of the following groups of expressions. Write the word on the line given.*

1. to relish, love, admire, esteem _____

2. sleepy, inattentive, unobservant _____

3. undistinguished, unremarkable; unknown _____

4. subsequent, later, ensuing, following _____

5. properly, as it should be, in order _____

6. favor, approval, pleasure, blessing _____

7. petty, piddling, trifling, inconsequential _____

8. a pro, past master, expert, veteran _____

9. incompetent, inept, unskilled, ignorant _____

10. to reassure, put at ease, soothe, quiet _____

11. foreign, alien; wild, untamed _____

12. to know for sure, know for certain _____

13. faultlessness, perfection _____

14. to neglect, ignore; to discourage, hinder _____

15. hindmost, last; secondary _____

Choosing the Right Word

*Encircle the **boldface** word that more satisfactorily completes each of the following sentences.*

1. She may have given wrong information in court, but this was an honest mistake and certainly does not make her guilty of (**perjury, wrath**).

2. I am disturbed by the (**momentum, paradox**) of impoverished people in the richest land on earth.

3. No parent can ever be (**vigilant, amiss**) enough to prevent a small child from taking many a painful tumble.

4. Since there had been no (**prior, proficient**) notice of the scholarship competition, we had practically no time to prepare for it.

5. It was hard to believe that the small, rather ordinary-looking person who was standing before us was a world-famous (**notable, fledgling**).

6. To say that the U.S. Constitution is one of the greatest documents of all time does not mean that it is entirely without (**momentum, flaws**).

7. I can forgive an honest mistake, but I (**presume, detest**) any attempt to cover up errors by lying.

8. The charges of incompetence the candidate leveled at her opponent were but the opening (**brawl, salvo**) in her campaign to become mayor.

9. Please don't take it (**amiss, notably**) if I suggest that your French accent sounds more like Paris, Texas, than Paris, France.

10. The rather skinny boy whom we had noticed only two years before as a (**prior, fledgling**) quarterback was now an all-American!

11. Abraham Lincoln had very little formal schooling, but his mind was (**nurtured, flawed**) by such great works as the Bible and Shakespeare.

12. Under the American system of justice, any person accused of a crime is (**presumed, flawed**) to be innocent until proven guilty.

13. Though I hadn't expected to be treated quite so unkindly by the audience, I didn't become (**flustered, nurtured**) or lose my professional cool.

14. The easternmost tip of Cuba was the first populated area in the region to feel the (**paradox, wrath**) of Hurricane Zelda.

15. As support for our candidate continued to gain (**momentum, salvo**), it soon became clear that he would win the election by a landslide.

16. Her happy (**domestic, nurture**) life gives her a great deal of relief from the everyday strains of running a large company.

17. *Romeo and Juliet* opens with members of the rival houses of Montague and Capulet (**brawling, perjuring**) like drunkards in the streets of Verona.

18. She worked so easily and quietly that at first we did not realize quite how remarkably (**proficient, amiss**) she was in the laboratory.

19. (**Foremost, Flagrant**) among the reasons that so many millions of immigrants have come to the United States is the desire for freedom.

20. How can you expect the court to excuse your repeated and (**flagrant, vigilant**) violations of the traffic laws?

Unit 8

Definitions *Note carefully the spelling, pronunciation, and definition of each of the following words. Then write the word in the blank space in the illustrative phrase following.*

1. **abnormal**
(ab 'nôr məl)
(*adj.*) not usual, not typical, strange
an _____ situation

2. **capsize**
('kap sīz)
(*v.*) to turn bottom side up, upset
_____ a boat

3. **catastrophe**
(kə 'tas trə fē)
(*n.*) a large-scale disaster, misfortune, or failure
a nuclear _____

4. **decrease**
(*v.*, di 'krēs;
n., 'dē krēs)
(*v.*) to become or make less; (*n.*) a lessening
_____ in size

5. **disputatious**
(dis pyü 'tā shəs)
(*adj.*) inclined to argue or debate; provoking debate
_____ baseball fans

6. **eject**
(i 'jekt)
(*v.*) to drive or throw out, evict
_____ the troublesome spectator

7. **flourish**
('flər ish)
(*v.*) to grow, thrive, be prosperous; to wave in the air; (*n.*) a dramatic gesture; a fanfare of horns
as long as the business _____

8. **incentive**
(in 'sen tiv)
(*n.*) a reason for doing something; something that stimulates action
an _____ to learn

9. **insubordinate**
(in sə 'bôrd ən ət)
(*adj.*) disobedient, rebellious
an _____ junior officer

10. **legible**
('lej ə bəl)
(*adj.*) easily read
handwriting that is _____

11. **nub**
(nəb)
(*n.*) the central point or heart of a matter; a knob
the _____ of the argument

12. **onslaught**
('än slôt)
(*n.*) a violent attack; a sudden rush of something
the _____ of winter

13. **ordain**
(ôr 'dān)
(*v.*) to establish by law; to order or command; to appoint as a priest or minister; to destine
_____ by fate

14. **outstrip**
(aut 'strip)
(*v.*) to get ahead of, do better than, exceed
_____ their rivals

15. **pervade**
(pər 'vād)
(*v.*) to spread throughout
_____ the atmosphere

16. prudent
('prüd ənt)
(*adj.*) cautious, careful, showing good sense
_____ investments

17. quench
(kwench)
(*v.*) to put out, extinguish, end
_____ the flames

18. remnant
('rem nənt)
(*n.*) a small part remaining behind
the _____ of the army

19. simultaneous
(sī məl 'tā nē əs)
(*adj.*) happening or existing at the same time
a _____ translation of a speech

20. swerve
(swərv)
(*v.*) to turn aside sharply; (*n.*) a sharp or sudden turn
_____ sharply to the right

Completing the Sentence

Choose the word from this unit that best completes each of the following sentences. Write the word in the space provided.

1. By landing the damaged plane in an open field, the pilot prevented a

major _____ from occurring.

2. My brother was _____ a priest after he had completed his studies at the seminary.

3. When a deer suddenly ran out onto the road, the car _____ quickly to avoid hitting it.

4. When my canoe unexpectedly hit a tree stump and _____ ,
I suddenly found myself neck-deep in some very cold and dirty water.

5. At the first shock of the enemy's _____ , our lines wavered a bit, but they soon recovered and held firm.

6. Even the most _____ businessperson knows that there are times when it is necessary to take chances.

7. The writing on the curious old document had faded badly, but it was still

perfectly _____ when held up to the light.

8. After our team won the last big game of the season, we all ran out onto the

field, _____ our pennants and banners jubilantly.

9. As the holidays approached, a feeling of excitement and anticipation

seemed to _____ the entire school.

10. "If that _____ young hothead had followed my orders to the letter," the general remarked sourly, "we wouldn't be in this fix!"

11. American farms continue to produce more and more food, even though the number of people working them has actually _____ .

12. Although we are used to severe winters, a heavy snowfall this early in the season is quite _____ .

13. Let's ignore minor side issues and get to the _____ of the problem as quickly as possible.

14. The only thing that ever really _____ my thirst on a stifling summer afternoon is a glass of ice-cold lemonade.

15. When you want to remove the cassette from the tape deck, just push this button, and the cartridge will _____ automatically.

16. The secret of the trick is to remove the first card and pick up the second so quickly that the two actions seem to be _____ .

17. After I had eaten my fill, I threw the _____ of my dinner into my dog's dish.

18. Do you really believe that making money is the only _____ that leads people to work hard and try to excel?

19. Though we are still the leading producers of various industrial products, other countries are catching up fast and may soon _____ us.

20. Trying to avoid an argument with that _____ fellow is like trying to nail oatmeal to the wall.

Synonyms   *Choose the word from this unit that is most nearly **the same** in meaning as each of the following groups of expressions. Write the word on the line given.*

1. the core, heart, kernel, nucleus, crux   _____

2. to outdo, outperform, outdistance, surpass   _____

3. a stimulus, spur, motive, inducement   _____

4. to turn aside, veer, digress, sheer off   _____

5. to prosper, thrive, burgeon   _____

6. argumentative, quarrelsome, contentious   _____

7. to evict, oust, expel, kick out   _____

8. occurring at one and the same time   _____

9. a disaster, calamity, tragedy, cataclysm   _____

10. readable, clear, decipherable   _____

11. cautious, wary; sensible, judicious ——————————

12. freakish, unnatural, irregular, anomalous ——————————

13. to extinguish, douse, stifle; to slake ——————————

14. to overturn, upset, upend, tip over ——————————

15. a remainder, residue, leftover, fragment ——————————

16. to anoint, consecrate; to enact, decree ——————————

17. to lessen, reduce, dwindle, diminish ——————————

18. to saturate, permeate, diffuse, imbue ——————————

19. an assault, charge, foray; an onset ——————————

20. defiant, unruly, rebellious, mutinous ——————————

Antonyms *Choose the word from this unit that is most nearly **opposite** in meaning to each of the following groups of expressions. Write the word on the line given.*

1. to trail, lag behind, bring up the rear ——————————

2. to increase, grow, develop, wax ——————————

3. unreadable, indecipherable ——————————

4. to ignite, kindle, set on fire ——————————

5. obedient, submissive, docile, tractable ——————————

6. foolish, unwise; rash, reckless ——————————

7. the fringe, the periphery, the edge ——————————

8. to stay on the straight and narrow ——————————

9. a curb, check, restraint, hindrance ——————————

10. to wither, die, fade, shrivel up ——————————

11. to admit, let in; to insert ——————————

12. normal, usual, regular, typical ——————————

13. a triumph, victory, success ——————————

14. occurring at different times ——————————

15. to remain upright ——————————

16. nonargumentative, peaceable, pacific ——————————

17. to forbid, veto, cancel ——————————

8

Choosing the Right Word   *Encircle the* **boldface** *word that more satisfactorily completes each of the following sentences.*

1. I'm following a very strict study schedule, but I must admit that I (**swerved, flourished**) from it when that big TV special came along.

2. When the musicians failed to arrive and the air-conditioning conked out, we realized that the party was becoming a (**nub, catastrophe**).

3. Even though you may think your supervisor is wrong, you won't be able to hold your job if you act (**simultaneously, insubordinately**).

4. As (**ordained, flourished**) in the U.S. Constitution, the President must be a native-born American at least 35 years old when he takes office.

5. Has the ability of human beings to produce new inventions (**quenched, outstripped**) their ability to use them wisely?

6. The first (**onslaught, remnant**) of the disease is marked by a severe fever and the appearance of an ugly rash all over the body.

7. Doesn't it seem (**abnormal, insubordinate**) for a bright young person to show no interest in taking part in any school activities?

8. When the elderly pianist began to play, we were saddened to observe that he had only a(n) (**incentive, remnant**) of his once great skill.

9. We have made some progress in cleaning up the slums in our community, but that is certainly no reason to (**decrease, eject**) our efforts.

10. The train and the car approached the crossing almost (**simultaneously, prudently**), and a terrible accident seemed unavoidable.

11. After the officials had put a stop to the fight that had broken out, they (**ejected, ordained**) the offending players from the game.

12. All our hopes and plans were (**capsized, outstripped**) when we learned that we would not be able to attend the music festival.

13. The only advice I can give you is to take the problems one at a time and deal with each in a sensible and (**prudent, disputatious**) way.

14. With eager students and able teachers, learning will (**flourish, decrease**), even though the school building may be old and shabby.

15. To get a good grade, make sure that your composition is interesting in content, correct in grammar and spelling, and (**abnormal, legible**).

16. As we returned to the dressing room after that terrible first half, the whole atmosphere seemed to be (**pervaded, capsized**) by defeat.

17. The high spirits with which we had begun the hike were soon (**pervaded, quenched**) when it began to rain.

18. The possibility of getting a summer job in an air-conditioned office is all the (**incentive, onslaught**) I need to improve my typing.

19. Two of the more (**abnormal, disputatious**) members of the committee soon got into an argument about where to build the new facility.

20. "We have become so engrossed in the minor details of the situation that we have left no time to consider the (**nub, incentive**) of the matter," I said.

Unit 9

Definitions

Note carefully the spelling, pronunciation, and definition of each of the following words. Then write the word in the blank space in the illustrative phrase following.

1. accelerate
(ak 'sel ə rāt)

(*v.*) to speed up, cause to move faster; to bring about more quickly

_____ our pace

2. bystander
('bī stan dər)

(*n.*) one who looks on or observes, a person present but not taking part

a group of curious _____

3. canvass
('kan vəs)

(*v.*) to go through an area in order to procure votes, sales, or opinions; to go over in detail; to discuss

_____ the neighborhood for support

4. casual
('kazh ə wəl)

(*adj.*) happening by chance or on an irregular basis; showing little concern; informal

a _____ remark

5. downtrodden
('daùn träd ən)

(*adj.*) treated unfairly and cruelly, oppressed

_____ masses longing to be free

6. entice
(en 'tīs)

(*v.*) to attract, tempt

_____ shoppers into the store

7. erode
(i 'rōd)

(*v.*) to wear away gradually, eat away

where the ground has been _____

8. flounder
('flaùn dər)

(*v.*) to thrash about in a clumsy or ineffective way

_____ about hopelessly for days

9. graphic
('graf ik)

(*adj.*) lifelike, vivid; relating to the pictorial arts

a _____ description

10. gruesome
('grü səm)

(*adj.*) horrible, revolting, ghastly

a _____ murder

11. melancholy
('mel ən käl ē)

(*adj.*) sad, gloomy, unhappy; (*n.*) sadness, gloominess

the _____ days of autumn

12. ordeal
(ôr 'dēl)

(*n.*) a difficult or painful experience, a trial

exhausted by the _____

13. parch
(pärch)

(*v.*) to make dry and thirsty; to shrivel with heat

left _____ by the drought

14. persist
(pər 'sist)

(*v.*) to continue steadily in a course of action, refuse to stop or be changed; to last, remain

_____ in their bad habits

15. puny
('pyü nē)

(*adj.*) of less than normal strength or size; weak, sickly; of no importance

a _____ opponent

16. quibble
('kwib əl)

(*v.*) to evade or belittle a point by twisting words or raising minor objections; (*n.*) a petty objection

_____ over details

17. ratify
('rat ə fī)

(*v.*) to approve, give formal approval to, confirm

_____ an amendment

18. regal
('rē gəl)

(*adj.*) royal, kinglike; fit for a king

a truly _____ gift

19. stifle
('stī fəl)

(*v.*) to smother, prevent from breathing; to hold back or choke off

_____ one's anger

20. vital
('vīt əl)

(*adj.*) having life, living; necessary to life, essential; key, crucial

a matter of _____ importance

Completing the Sentence

Choose the word from this unit that best completes each of the following sentences. Write it in the space given.

1. As we fought the forest fire, we were almost _____ by the extreme heat and heavy smoke.

2. According to Greek mythology, the Sirens used their remarkable singing voices to _____ unwary sailors to watery graves.

3. If you were spending your own money, rather than mine, you would be more inclined to _____ over the price of the repairs.

4. When the inexperienced swimmer realized that he was in really deep water, he panicked and began to _____ around wildly.

5. These immigrants were _____ in their native land, but in America they enjoy all the rights and privileges of free people.

6. Regular visits to the dentist are _____ if you wish to have healthy, good-looking teeth.

7. A group of reporters from the local TV station _____ our district for reactions to the proposed changes in the law.

8. How can he _____ in denying that he was at the scene of the crime when a number of people saw him there?

9. The sled _____ with alarming speed as it went down the steep slope.

10. The President's powers in foreign affairs are limited by the fact that any treaty he may negotiate must be _____ by the Senate.

11. After an hour of trudging along the dusty road under the hot sun, we were so _____ that all we could think of was cold water.

12. At that tender age I was so shy that I found it a(n) _____ to be introduced to people I'd never met before.

13. In our environment class, we learned that in much of the United States the topsoil has been badly _____ by natural forces.

14. The _____ sight that greeted my eyes at the scene of that awful traffic accident gave me nightmares for weeks.

15. Some poets are at their best when dealing with happy events, while others seem to prefer the more _____ side of life.

16. She gave us a clear, detailed, and _____ picture of what is likely to happen if we fail to come to grips with the pollution problem.

17. Since Deborah's party is by no means a formal affair, _____ clothing is in order.

18. He now claims that he was just an innocent _____ , but I saw him actually taking part in the fight.

19. As soon as he learned that he was to play the king in the play, his whole personality took on an almost _____ air.

20. Though the new halfback looked a little _____ to us, he managed to hold his own against players twice his size and build.

Synonyms   *Choose the word from this unit that is most nearly **the same** in meaning as each of the following groups of expressions. Write the word on the line given.*

1. to confirm, endorse, sanction, uphold   _____

2. vivid, lifelike, lively, colorful   _____

3. necessary, indispensable, crucial   _____

4. dejection, depression; depressed, dejected   _____

5. to dry up, dehydrate, desiccate   _____

6. to choke, strangle, smother, suppress   _____

7. accidental, haphazard; offhand; informal   _____

8. undersized, pint-size, small; weak   _____

9. ghastly, gory, hideous, grisly, horrible   _____

10. to keep going, persevere; to last, endure   _____

11. mistreated, oppressed, ground underfoot   _____

12. to wear away, corrode, abrade   _____

13. majestic, stately, princely, august   _____

14. to tempt, lure, beguile   _____

15. an observer, spectator, onlooker   _____

16. to nitpick, split hairs, cavil; to squabble   _____

17. to poll, survey; to solicit   _____

18. a trial, test, hardship   _____

19. to speed up, step up, quicken, hasten   _____

20. to thrash about, wallow; to struggle   _____

Antonyms   *Choose the word from this unit that is most nearly* ***opposite*** *in meaning to each of the following groups of expressions. Write the word on the line given.*

1. an active participant   _____

2. a pleasant experience, pleasure; a cinch   _____

3. joy, elation; merry, happy, cheerful   _____

4. to give up, discontinue, throw in the towel   _____

5. to cancel, repeal, annul, veto   _____

6. robust, brawny; mammoth, gigantic   _____

7. dull, boring; unrealistic; colorless   _____

8. to nauseate, sicken, revolt, repel   _____

9. nonessential, unnecessary   _____

10. to slow down, retard, decelerate   _____

11. to nurture, promote, encourage   _____

12. pleasant, delightful, appealing   _____

13. formal; serious; premeditated, intentional   _____

14. to soak, drench, saturate, waterlog   _____

15. lowly, humble, abject, servile   _____

16. uplifted, liberated, raised up from the dirt   _____

Choosing the Right Word   *Encircle the **boldface** word that more satisfactorily completes each of the following sentences.*

1. Instead of continuing to (**flounder**, accelerate) helplessly, we must decide on a goal and start to move toward it.

2. "How can you compare a free American worker," the factory owner asked, "to the (**downtrodden**, melancholy) serfs and slaves of earlier times?"

3. When I asked you what you meant by those words, I wasn't (**quibbling**, ratifying) but trying to discover what the problem was.

4. I find your offer most (gruesome, **enticing**), but my better judgment tells me to have nothing to do with it.

5. The dictator used fear and violence to (**stifle**, canvass) discontent among the people he ruled.

6. Do her efforts to (**accelerate**, flounder) our departure mean that she is trying to help us, or just get rid of us?

7. After weeks of no rain, the (**parched**, graphic) earth turned to dust that was blown away by the strong winds.

8. It is hard to believe that this sturdy, six-foot basketball star was a (vital, **puny**) 100-pounder only a few years ago.

9. The soundness of the basic ideas of the Constitution has been (**ratified**, enticed) by the experience of over 200 years.

10. In a democracy, the average citizen should be an active participant in public affairs, not just a quiet (**bystander**, enticer).

11. You will never do well in school so long as your attitude toward your studies remains (downtrodden, **casual**) and unconcerned.

12. No doubt he has our best interests at heart, but my faith in him has been (**eroded**, persisted) by repeated evidence of his poor judgment.

13. I think it showed bad judgment on your part to tell such a (**gruesome**, puny) story to a child who is so easily frightened.

14. She made what proved to be a (**vital**, parched) mistake when she gave the job to one of the applicants without checking his references.

15. The chairwoman of the department (**canvassed**, stifled) the entire faculty for ideas on how to put the new program into effect.

16. In spite of all the setbacks we have had, we must (**persist**, quibble) in our efforts to achieve the goal we have set for ourselves.

17. With her (**regal**, graphic) bearing and imperious manner Elizabeth I looked every inch the queen she in fact was.

18. If you have prepared properly for the exams, there will be no reason to regard them as a terrible (quibble, **ordeal**).

19. Aided by diagrams on the blackboard, she gave a summary of her plan so clear and (**graphic**, regal) that it won the full support of the audience.

20. In spite of the bright sunshine and the happy crowds, a strange mood of (ordeal, **melancholy**) seemed to take possession of me.

Analogies *In each of the following, encircle the item that best completes the comparison.*

1. **legible** is to **read** as
   a. audible is to see
   b. portable is to carry
   c. lovable is to detest
   d. notable is to write

2. **foreign** is to **domestic** as
   a. gruesome is to pleasant
   b. regal is to princely
   c. foremost is to backhanded
   d. simultaneous is to timely

3. **swerve** is to **sideways** as
   a. presume is to backwards
   b. erode is to inside out
   c. ordain is to forwards
   d. capsize is to upside down

4. **vigilant** is to **favorable** as
   a. notable is to unfavorable
   b. gruesome is to favorable
   c. disputatious is to unfavorable
   d. abnormal is to favorable

5. **insubordinate** is to **obedience** as
   a. prudent is to caution
   b. vigilant is to perception
   c. foremost is to position
   d. casual is to formality

6. **treaty** is to **ratify** as
   a. trust is to erode
   b. check is to countersign
   c. goal is to outstrip
   d. cane is to flourish

7. **eject** is to **expel** as
   a. presume is to know
   b. fluster is to disconcert
   c. canvass is to paint
   d. pervade is to avoid

8. **vital** is to **life** as
   a. amiss is to knowledge
   b. vigilant is to size
   c. graphic is to vividness
   d. gruesome is to concern

9. **accelerate** is to **faster** as
   a. decrease is to slower
   b. retard is to faster
   c. outstrip is to slower
   d. persist is to faster

10. **prudent** is to **wisdom** as
    a. legible is to sense
    b. honest is to perjury
    c. wrathful is to patience
    d. proficient is to skill

11. **quench** is to **wet** as
    a. capsize is to dry
    b. nurture is to wet
    c. parch is to dry
    d. flourish is to wet

12. **pygmy** is to **puny** as
    a. ogre is to flagrant
    b. giant is to colossal
    c. fledgling is to proficient
    d. bystander is to foremost

13. **disputatious** is to **quibble** as
    a. stubborn is to persist
    b. slow is to outstrip
    c. peaceful is to brawl
    d. wrathful is to canvass

14. **practice** is to **proficient** as
    a. experience is to talented
    b. dieting is to chubby
    c. ability is to sincere
    d. study is to knowledgeable

15. **prior** is to **before** as
    a. subsequent is to after
    b. simultaneous is to before
    c. amiss is to after
    d. flagrant is to before

16. **enraged** is to **wrath** as
    a. contented is to jealousy
    b. downtrodden is to joy
    c. detested is to interest
    d. depressed is to melancholy

17. **brawl** is to **war** as
    a. setback is to catastrophe
    b. movement is to momentum
    c. salvo is to salute
    d. withdrawal is to onslaught

18. **bystander** is to **observe** as
    a. fledgling is to instruct
    b. domestic is to referee
    c. activist is to participate
    d. paradox is to report

Synonyms *In each of the following groups, encircle the word or expression that is most nearly **the same** in meaning as the **boldface word** in the introductory phrase.*

1. **pervade** the air of the room
   a. pollute   b. fill   c. cleanse   d. breathe

2. **nub** of the problem
   a. author   b. cause   c. heart   d. result

3. **quench** the flames
   a. start   b. report   c. extinguish   d. observe

4. **regal** robes
   a. cheap   b. kingly   c. colorful   d. strange

5. be ever **vigilant**
   a. bold   b. timid   c. watchful   d. patriotic

6. **presume** their innocence
   a. suppose   b. deny   c. defend   d. discuss

7. **brawling** in the streets
   a. playing   b. standing   c. loitering   d. fighting

8. **eroded** his determination
   a. increased   b. wore away   c. explained   d. justified

9. **outstrip** my rivals
   a. beat   b. lose to   c. criticize   d. describe

10. **downtrodden** masses
    a. oppressed   b. foreign   c. hardworking   d. ignorant

11. harrowing **ordeal**
    a. scene   b. idea   c. trial   d. responsibility

12. **onslaught** of the disease
    a. onset   b. cure   c. end   d. symptom

13. has gone **amiss**
    a. properly   b. well   c. wrong   d. slowly

14. **stifle** a yawn
    a. notice   b. suppress   c. cause   d. produce

15. provide some **incentive** to improve
    a. help   b. direction   c. solution   d. inducement

16. could not find a **flaw**
    a. defect   b. clue   c. friend   d. reason

Shades of Meaning *Read each sentence carefully. Then encircle the item that best completes the statement below the sentence.*

According to the principle of Manifest Destiny — first advanced in the 1840s — the United States was ordained to expand westward to the Pacific.   **(2)**

1. In line 2 the word **ordained** is used to mean
   a. ordered   b. appointed   c. enacted   d. fated

Far from being only casual acquaintances, as they claimed, the two had
secretly been in cahoots for years. (2)

2. The word **casual** in line 1 most nearly means
a. occasional   b. personal   c. unconcerned   d. accidental

Heavy losses during the Battle of Britain forced the Royal Air Force
sometimes to send fledglings up against the German formations. (2)

3. In line 2 the word **fledglings** is best defined as
a. young birds   c. veteran flyers
b. novice pilots   d. damaged fighters

"There will be no response to the proposal," remarked the diplomat, "until
my government has had an opportunity to canvass the terms and
conditions." (2)

4. The best definition for the word **canvass** in line 2 is
a. gather   c. examine
b. solicit   d. poll

I think that the chairperson is doing me an injustice by dismissing my
contribution to the project as "puny." (2)

5. The word **puny** in line 2 most nearly means
a. sickly   c. undersized
b. unimportant   d. off the wall

Antonyms   *In each of the following groups, encircle the word or
expression that is most nearly* **opposite** *in meaning to
the* **boldface word** *in the introductory phrase.*

1. detest snobs
a. adore   b. notice   c. avoid   d. loathe

2. prudent shoppers
a. sensible   b. wealthy   c. demanding   d. foolish

3. my parents' **wrath**
a. favor   b. intelligence   c. position   d. anger

4. notable teacher
a. experienced   b. up-to-date   c. unimpressive   d. demanding

5. legible handwriting
a. elegant   b. unreadable   c. childish   d. neat

6. flagrant offense
a. youthful   b. minor   c. serious   d. unexplained

7. foremost among the candidates
a. chief   b. last   c. first   d. most popular

8. vital issues
a. unimportant   b. interesting   c. difficult   d. life-or-death

9. abnormal situation
a. strange   b. new   c. interesting   d. commonplace

10. fledgling dentist
  a. veteran   b. wealthy   c. painless   d. clumsy

11. melancholy state of mind
  a. sleepy   b. sad   c. happy   d. weird

12. proficient swimmer
  a. fast   b. unskilled   c. expert   d. fearless

13. decrease in scope
  a. shrivel   b. dwindle   c. change   d. grow

14. puny for their size
  a. brawny   b. wise   c. intelligent   d. small

15. ratify an agreement
  a. honor   b. cancel   c. write   d. endorse

Completing the Sentence

From the following words, choose the one that best completes each of the sentences below. Write the word in the space provided.

Group A

persist	eject	quench	flourish
gruesome	salvo	outstrip	flaw
quibble	brawl	disputatious	nub

1. Although my new invention still has a few _____ in it, they are not beyond correction.

2. Let's cut all the fancy talk and get down to the _____ of the matter.

3. Oranges, lemons, and other citrus fruits do not grow in the Arctic, but they _____ in the tropics.

4. Since she has spent several summer vacations in France, it is not at all surprising that she _____ her classmates in her ability to speak French.

5. I was not prepared for the _____ sight that met my eyes at the scene of that horrible disaster.

Group B

amiss	remnant	presume	bystander
catastrophe	flounder	vital	prior
domestic	proficient	parch	melancholy

1. You _____ too much when you take it for granted that I will support you for Class President.

R

2. Although I had no _____ knowledge of his background, I soon realized that he was an expert mechanic.

3. When the librarian saw me _____ helplessly in trying to gather material for my research paper, she offered to assist me.

4. Instead of always being a(n) _____ at athletic events, why don't you take part in some of them?

5. If you were as _____ at your schoolwork as you are at chess, you would be a straight-A student.

Word Families

A. *On the line provided, write a **noun form** of each of the following words.*

EXAMPLE: persist — **persistence**

1. proficient _____
2. prior _____
3. flagrant _____
4. ratify _____
5. detest _____
6. vigilant _____
7. presume _____
8. erode _____
9. entice _____
10. abnormal _____
11. eject _____
12. insubordinate _____
13. legible _____
14. prudent _____
15. simultaneous _____
16. accelerate _____
17. gruesome _____
18. puny _____
19. vital _____
20. ordain _____

B. *On the line provided, write a **verb** related to each of the following words.*

EXAMPLE: pervasive — **pervade**

1. notable _____

2. perjury _____

3. domestic _____

4. vital _____

5. disputatious _____

**Filling
the Blanks**   *Encircle the pair of words that best complete the
meaning of each of the following passages.*

1. My throat became so _____ during that long trek over
dusty trails on the hottest day of summer that I firmly believed nothing
would ever _____ my thirst!

   a. flawed . . . nurture   c. parched . . . quench
   b. puny . . . decrease   d. flagrant . . . pervade

2. "An experienced worker doesn't usually have trouble handling a new
job with _____ ," the personnel manager observed. "A
beginner, however, will normally _____ around until he
or she learns the ropes."

   a. prudence . . . quibble   c. incentive . . . flourish
   b. proficiency . . . flounder   d. vigilance . . . swerve

3. If you want to stop your automobile, apply the brakes. If you want it to gain
_____ , step on the _____ .

   a. momentum . . . accelerator   c. wrath . . . flaw
   b. salvo . . . nub   d. incentive . . . paradox

4. "It isn't _____ to spend more than you make," I observed.
"Only a fool would allow expenses to _____ income."

   a. vital . . . fluster   c. abnormal . . . nurture
   b. amiss . . . stifle   d. prudent . . . outstrip

5. When prices go up, the value of our money _____ . The
higher the cost of living climbs, the more deeply inflation _____
away the purchasing power of the dollar.

   a. accelerates . . . entices   c. persists . . . perjures
   b. decreases . . . erodes   d. flourishes . . . parches

6. As we _____ violently to the right to avoid some rocks that
suddenly sprang into view, our canoe _____ and pitched us
headlong into the churning waters of the river.

   a. flourished . . . flustered   c. swerved . . . capsized
   b. canvassed . . . ejected   d. brawled . . . nurtured

Analogies   *In each of the following, encircle the item that best completes the comparison.*

1. perjury is to **lie** as
a. forgery is to kidnap
b. robbery is to cheat
c. larceny is to envy
d. homicide is to kill

2. counterfeit is to **inimitable** as
a. douse is to inflammable
b. replace is to indispensable
c. continue is to interminable
d. see is to inaudible

3. plague is to **catastrophe** as
a. operation is to entertainment
b. vacation is to danger
c. cross-examination is to ordeal
d. appointment is to emergency

4. foretaste is to **preview** as
a. luster is to radiance
b. recompense is to ingredient
c. salvo is to snare
d. iota is to nub

5. paradox is to **bewilder** as
a. pleasure is to wince
b. failure is to animate
c. triumph is to brood
d. mishap is to fluster

6. drought is to **parched** as
a. deluge is to sodden
b. blizzard is to transparent
c. trickle is to drench
d. heat wave is to unscathed

7. eradicate is to **nurture** as
a. germinate is to flourish
b. browse is to maul
c. stifle is to foster
d. dupe is to hoodwink

8. incentive is to **goad** as
a. potential is to mortify
b. quibble is to dishearten
c. flaw is to entice
d. hazard is to dissuade

9. notable is to **prominent** as
a. tactful is to spirited
b. barren is to void
c. graphic is to simultaneous
d. sullen is to poised

10. substantial is to **weight** as
a. dynamic is to momentum
b. trivial is to importance
c. makeshift is to solidity
d. marginal is to leeway

Shades of Meaning   *Read each sentence carefully. Then encircle the item that best completes the statement below the sentence.*

In the plays of Shakespeare, the entrance of a king is often announced by a flourish of trumpets. (2)

1. In line 2 the word **flourish** most nearly means
a. prosperity   b. gesture   c. waving   d. fanfare

Try as they might, negotiators could not persuade the hostile parties to sit down and talk, much less patch up their differences. (2)

2. The word **hostile** in line 1 is best defined as
a. warring   b. unfavorable   c. suspicious   d. restless

The gunnery officer concluded the drill by ordering the launching crew to fire a missile at a drone. (2)

3. In line 2 the word **drone** is used to mean
a. swarm of bees
b. remote-control target
c. loud humming noise
d. loafer

Though Lee's surrender brought to an end the terrible bloodshed of the Civil War, hard feelings between North and South persisted for generations. **(2)**

4. The best definition for the word **persisted** in line 2 is
a. were unchanged
b. slowly disappeared
c. stubbornly endured
d. flared up

"May I presume upon your patience," I inquired of my boss, "to ask you to explain once again why I can't have that raise?" **(2)**

5. In line 1 the phrase **presume upon** most nearly means
a. safely assume
b. take liberties with
c. dare
d. completely exhaust

Filling the Blanks   *Encircle the pair of words that best complete the meaning of each of the following passages.*

1. The violence of the enemy's _____ at first threatened to turn our position and drive us from the field, but we quickly regrouped and _____ a stunning defeat on the foe.
a. vengeance . . . entreated
b. onslaught . . . inflicted
c. wrath . . . eroded
d. remnant . . . consolidated

2. The little camper's _____ expression and mournful voice told me more eloquently than words could ever have just how much she _____ for home.
a. fickle . . . canvassed
b. anonymous . . . scurried
c. melancholy . . . yearned
d. prudent . . . catered

3. When the police _____ the man about his movements on the fatal night, he claimed to have been nowhere near the scene of the crime. So far, however, law enforcement officials have been completely unable to _____ his alibi, and the fellow remains the chief suspect in the case.
a. indulged . . . ratify
b. ordained . . . swerve
c. canvassed . . . pelt
d. interrogated . . . verify

4. Sometimes, public opinion is so _____ and unpredictable that a candidate who is the darling of the crowd one day may find himself or herself roundly _____ the next.
a. fickle . . . detested
b. miscellaneous . . . presumed
c. proficient . . . prescribed
d. orthodox . . . dominated

5. The study of history teaches us that laziness and indifference may slowly _____ away the rights and privileges of a free people. For that reason, we must be ever _____ in protecting and defending our liberties.
a. hurtle . . . transparent
b. erode . . . vigilant
c. eradicate . . . docile
d. nurture . . . tactful

Unit 10

Definitions   *Note carefully the spelling, pronunciation, and definition of each of the following words. Then write the word in the blank space in the illustrative phrase following.*

1. **bellow**
   ('bel ō)

   (v.) to make a sound similar to that of a bull, roar; (n.) a loud, angry roar

   _____ in pain

2. **beneficiary**
   (ben ə 'fish ē er ē)

   (n.) one who benefits from something; a person who is left money or other property in a will or the like

   the chief _____ of the will

3. **botch**
   (bäch)

   (v.) to repair or patch poorly; make a mess of; (n.) a hopelessly bungled job

   _____ the report badly

4. **clutter**
   ('klət ər)

   (v.) to fill or cover in a disorderly way; (n.) state of disorder, mess

   _____ up the room

5. **dilapidated**
   (də 'lap ə dā tid)

   (adj.) falling apart or ruined, run-down

   a _____ house

6. **dismantle**
   (dis 'man təl)

   (v.) to take apart; to strip of something

   _____ a ship

7. **farce**
   (färs)

   (n.) a play filled with ridiculous or absurd happenings; broad or far-fetched humor; a ridiculous sham

   made a _____ of the election

8. **futile**
   ('fyüt əl)

   (adj.) not successful, failing to have any result; useless; unimportant, frivolous

   a _____ effort to save the child

9. **grueling**
   ('grü liŋ)

   (adj.) very tiring, calling for an extreme effort

   a _____ race

10. **hospitable**
    (häs 'pit ə bəl)

    (adj.) offering friendly or generous treatment to guests; open to anything new or strange

    _____ surroundings

11. **lair**
    (lâr)

    (n.) the home or den of a wild animal; any hideout

    trap the smugglers in their _____

12. **lavish**
    ('lav ish)

    (adj.) overly generous, extravagant; abundant; (v.) to spend or give freely or without limit

    _____ wedding gifts

13. **morbid**
    ('môr bid)

    (adj.) in an unhealthy mental state, extremely gloomy; caused by or related to disease, unwholesome

    take a _____ interest in the crime

14. notorious
(nō 'tôr ē əs)

(*adj.*) widely known because of bad conduct

a _____ bank robber

15. pamper
('pam pər)

(*v.*) to allow too many privileges, be too generous and easygoing toward

_____ one's children

16. parasite
('par ə sīt)

(*n.*) an organism that lives in or on another organism; one who lives off another person

lice and other _____

17. shirk
(shərk)

(*v.*) to avoid or get out of doing work, neglect a duty; to sneak, slink

to _____ a responsibility

18. surplus
('sər pləs)

(*n.*) an amount beyond what is required, excess; (*adj.*) more than what is needed or expected

_____ cash

19. timidity
(tə 'mid ə tē)

(*n.*) the state of being easily frightened

a shy child's natural _____

20. veto
('vē tō)

(*n.*) the power to forbid or prevent; (*v.*) to prohibit, reject

_____ a bill

Completing the Sentence

Choose the word for this unit that best completes each of the following sentences. Write the word in the space provided.

1. I know what it is that I have to do, and you may be certain that I will not _____ my duty.

2. Though the cabin was a little _____ when we bought it, we were able to spruce it up without going to a great deal of expense.

3. He is such a(n) _____ liar that no one takes anything he says seriously anymore.

4. Mr. and Mrs. Guarneri are such _____ people that we are always completely at ease whenever we visit them.

5. Since the defendant was never given a chance to prove his innocence, his so-called "trial" was nothing more than a(n) _____ .

6. The President can _____ a measure passed by a majority of Congress, but his _____ may be overridden.

7. It is hard to believe that a teenager so courageous and able on a camping trip can show so much _____ when invited to a dance.

8. The inexperienced typist _____ the letter he was trying to type and had to do it all over again.

9. The practice session was so _____ that we scarcely had the strength to get to the dressing room and take our showers.

10. Many people both here and abroad seem to have a(n) _____ fascination with the tragic fate of the Russian royal family.

11. As a child she was so _____ by her parents that she still seems to think that her wishes should be instantly granted.

12. The animals in the zoo are kept in quarters that are designed to imitate their _____ in the wild state.

13. Ever since the new tax laws went into effect, there has been speculation as to who the real _____ of the changes will be.

14. It is a curious fact of nature that most _____ are unable to survive when they are separated from the organisms they feed on.

15. When he realized that he had been tricked by his opponent, he let out a(n) _____ of rage that could be heard all over the gym.

16. The _____ food produced each year in the United States is desperately needed to feed hungry people all over the world.

17. When I accepted the invitation to the "strike party" after the play closed, I didn't realize that I had agreed to help _____ the sets.

18. They gave me so _____ a helping of dinner that for the first time in my life I was unable to polish off my plate.

19. Unfortunately, the brave lifeguard's valiant attempts to rescue the drowning swimmer proved _____ .

20. Why must you _____ up your mind with so many trivial and useless scraps of information?

Synonyms Choose the word from this unit that is most nearly **the same** in meaning as each of the following groups of expressions. Write the word on the line given.

1. run-down, in disrepair, gone to seed   _____

2. very generous, extravagant, excessive   _____

3. to try to avoid, duck, sidestep   _____

4. fruitless, vain, ineffective   _____

5. fearfulness, faintheartedness   _____

6. to take apart, disassemble, strip   _____

7. to reject, turn down, nix, forbid   _____

8. to mess up, foul up, bungle, mangle   _____

9. to coddle, cater to, indulge　　　　　　_____

10. gracious, friendly, cordial, courteous　　_____

11. an excess, glut, surfeit, overage　　　　_____

12. litter; disorder, confusion　　　　　　_____

13. a low comedy, buffoonery; a sham　　　_____

14. tiring, exhausting, punishing, taxing　　_____

15. disgraceful, infamous, disreputable　　_____

16. a den, nest, hideout　　　　　　　　_____

17. a recipient, heir　　　　　　　　　　_____

18. gloomy, depressed; unhealthy, unwholesome _____

19. a sponger, freeloader, leech　　　　　_____

20. to roar, yell, bawl, howl, holler　　　　_____

Antonyms　　　　*Choose the word from this unit that is most nearly*
__opposite__ in meaning to each of the following groups of
expressions. Write the word on the line given.

1. to put together, assemble, construct　　_____

2. to approve, endorse, ratify, confirm　　_____

3. wholesome, healthy; cheerful, blithe　　_____

4. easy, effortless, not taxing　　　　　　_____

5. order, tidiness, neatness　　　　　　　_____

6. to whisper, murmur, speak softly　　　_____

7. a tragedy; a melodrama, tearjerker　　_____

8. successful, effective　　　　　　　　_____

9. unfriendly, cold, icy, chilly　　　　　　_____

10. fearlessness, boldness, intrepidity　　_____

11. shipshape, trim, in good repair　　　　_____

12. stingy, meager; to begrudge, stint, deny _____

13. to abuse, maltreat, mistreat; to discipline _____

14. a shortage, lack, dearth, paucity　　　_____

15. unknown, obscure; respectable　　　　_____

16. to fulfill, perform, shoulder, take on　_____

Choosing the Right Word *Encircle the **boldface** word that more satisfactorily completes each of the following sentences.*

1. Since I was led to believe that she would approve my proposal, I was very much taken aback when it was (**lavished, vetoed**) out of hand.

2. The courts of many Renaissance princes were jammed with (**parasites, lairs**), toadies, and other idle hangers-on.

3. She was indeed fortunate to find herself working under a person who was (**notorious, hospitable**) to her revolutionary new ideas.

4. My experience has been that a person who cuts corners on small matters will also (**shirk, botch**) important responsibilities.

5. The modern TV sitcom developed out of the type of broad (**surplus, farce**) that slapstick comedians served up in the 1920's and 1930's.

6. Beneath the (**dismantled, dilapidated**) body of the getaway car, there was a powerful, finely tuned motor, capable of reaching high speeds.

7. I sometimes think that he enjoys being sick and having everyone wait on him, sympathize with him, and (**shirk, pamper**) him.

8. The best way to avoid those (**grueling, bellowing**) cram sessions just before the exams is to do your work steadily all term long.

9. When I think back to my days of basic training, I can almost hear the drill sergeant (**pampering, bellowing**) commands across the field.

10. After buying all the supplies for the club party, we were delighted to find that we had a grand (**surplus, veto**) of 65 cents.

11. When he said he would "beard the lion in his (**lair, clutter**)," he merely meant that he was going to have it out with the boss.

12. It would be impossible to (**pamper, dismantle**) our system of governmental checks and balances without destroying American democracy.

13. He amazed us by reaching into the pile of (**clutter, lair**) on his desk and pulling out exactly the piece of paper he wanted.

14. Their record is 100% consistent—they have managed to (**botch, clutter**) every job they have undertaken.

15. Even the toughest critics have been (**lavish, dilapidated**) in their praise of the new movie.

16. Ever since I was bitten by a stray mutt, I have had a (**morbid, lavish**) fear of dogs.

17. The campaign to eliminate pollution will prove (**futile, grueling**) unless it has the understanding and full cooperation of the public.

18. We who live in America today are the chief (**beneficiaries, parasites**) of the rich heritage of freedom left us by the Founding Fathers.

19. What a difference between the (**timidity, farce**) of the typical freshman and the know-it-all confidence of a senior!

20. He is (**hospitable, notorious**) for his habit of taking small loans from his friends and then conveniently forgetting about them.

Unit 11

Definitions
Note carefully the spelling, pronunciation, and definition of each of the following words. Then write the word in the blank space in the illustrative phrase following.

1. adequate
('ad ə kwət)
(*adj.*) sufficient, enough
_____ time for the task

2. ajar
(ə 'jär)
(*adj., adv.*) partly open
left the gate _____

3. dialogue
('dī ə läg)
(*n.*) a conversation between two or more people; an interchange of opinions and ideas, free discussion
the _____ in a play

4. emblem
('em bləm)
(*n.*) a symbol, sign, token
our school _____

5. gigantic
(jī 'gan tik)
(*adj.*) huge, giant, immense
a _____ hole in the ground

6. havoc
('hav ək)
(*n.*) very great destruction, ruin; great confusion and disorder
create _____ in the office

7. hearth
(härth)
(*n.*) the floor of a fireplace; the fireside as a symbol of the home and family
sitting by the _____

8. implore
(im 'plôr)
(*v.*) to beg earnestly for
_____ the judge to show mercy

9. infamous
('in fə məs)
(*adj.*) very wicked; disgraceful, shameful
_____ deeds

10. innumerable
(i 'nüm ə rə bəl)
(*adj.*) too many to count, without number
_____ complaints

11. lax
(laks)
(*adj.*) not strict, careless; lacking discipline; not tense, relaxed
a _____ attitude

12. mar
(mär)
(*v.*) to spoil, damage, injure
_____ the surface of the table

13. misdemeanor
(mis di 'mē nər)
(*n.*) a crime or offense that is less serious than a felony; any minor misbehavior or misconduct
fined for a _____

14. mull
(məl)
(*v.*) to think about, ponder; to grind or mix; to heat and flavor with spices
_____ over the situation

15. narrative
('nar ə tiv)

(*n.*) a story, detailed report; (*adj.*) having the quality or the nature of a story

a _____ of her life

16. overture
('ō vər ch
ur)

(*n.*) an opening move toward negotiation or action; a proposal or offer; an introductory section or part

the _____ to an opera

17. pact
(pakt)

(*n.*) an agreement, treaty

a mutual defense _____

18. stalemate
('stāl māt)

(*n.*) a situation in which further action by either of two opponents is impossible; (*v.*) to bring to a standstill

ended in _____

19. vindictive
(vin 'dik tiv)

(*adj.*) bearing a grudge, feeling or showing a strong tendency toward revenge

a _____ person

20. wilt
(wilt)

(*v.*) to become limp and drooping (as a flower), wither; to lose strength and vigor

when the flowers _____

Completing the Sentence

Choose the word from this unit that best completes each of the following sentences. Write the word in the space provided.

1. Since I have never done him any harm, I don't understand why he should

take such a(n) _____ attitude toward me.

2. Let me have some time to _____ over your proposal before I give you a definite answer.

3. Who has not gazed with awe at the _____ stars that fill the sky on a clear summer night!

4. Before you leave, be absolutely sure that your supplies of food and water

are _____ for an eight-day journey across the desert.

5. Can any punishment be too severe for someone who has been guilty of

such a(n) _____ crime?

6. You cannot discipline a group of teenagers by making a capital offense of

every _____ .

7. "The Highwayman" by Alfred Noyes is a(n) _____ poem that tells the story of a woman who sacrifices her life for her sweetheart.

8. Though my sister started out looking as fresh as a daisy, she began to

_____ noticeably after only five minutes in that heat.

9. Because the front door was _____ , the cat walked calmly into the living room.

10. No one questions the honesty and good intentions of the mayor, but he has been criticized for being _____ in carrying out his duties.

11. The dove is often used as a(n) _____ of peace.

12. The U.S. entry into World War I broke the _____ on the Western Front and tipped the balance in favor of an Allied victory.

13. The smoke from the logs burning on the _____ curled slowly upward into the chimney.

14. On our trip to California, we felt very small and unimportant as we stood beside the _____ redwood tree.

15. In most operettas, the musical numbers are connected to one another by spoken _____ .

16. Though some of Verdi's operas begin with short preludes, for others he composed full-length _____ .

17. One careless mistake can seriously _____ an otherwise perfect record.

18. Though Hitler's Germany and Stalin's Russia were bitter enemies, the two countries signed a nonaggression _____ in 1939.

19. She _____ the doctor to tell her frankly how badly her son had been hurt.

20. The flood had wrought such _____ that the governor of the state declared the stricken region a disaster area.

Synonyms   *Choose the word from this unit that is most nearly **the same** in meaning as each of the following groups of expressions. Write the word on the line given.*

1. vengeful, spiteful, malicious   _____

2. a fireplace; a chimney corner   _____

3. to injure, scar, disfigure, deface   _____

4. to sag, droop, wither, shrivel up   _____

5. to beg, entreat, beseech   _____

6. a deadlock, standoff, draw   _____

7. a badge, insignia; a symbol, token, sign   _____

8. enormous, immense, colossal, giant   _____

9. a prelude; an offer, tender, proposal

10. a treaty, compact, alliance; a deal

11. a conversation, discussion, exchange of ideas

12. slack, careless, negligent, remiss

13. sufficient, enough, satisfactory

14. a misdeed, petty offense or transgression

15. countless, beyond reckoning

16. a tale, story, chronicle

17. partly open

18. scandalous, villainous, flagrant, heinous

19. devastation, destruction, ruin, harm

20. to consider, reflect on, ponder

Antonyms   *Choose the word from this unit that is most nearly **opposite** in meaning to each of the following groups of expressions. Write the word on the line given.*

1. tiny, infinitesimal, diminutive

2. strict, vigilant, conscientious, scrupulous

3. insufficient, not enough, too little

4. closed tight, shut; open wide

5. countable; few in number

6. forgiving, relenting

7. a monologue, soliloquy

8. to beautify, embellish; to repair

9. glorious, splendid, illustrious; praiseworthy

10. to demand forcefully, clamor for

11. a felony, serious crime

12. peace and quiet, calm, order

13. to flourish, bloom, sprout; to perk up, revive

14. a finale; a postlude

15. a victory; a defeat

16. not to give something a second thought

Choosing the Right Word *Encircle the **boldface** word that more satisfactorily completes each of the following sentences.*

1. Contract talks have been stalled for weeks, and nothing either side has suggested can seem to break the (**stalemate, dialogue**).

2. Since I am willing to contribute to any worthy cause, there is no need to (**wilt, implore**) me for aid in such an emotional way.

3. After World War II the United States was not (**vindictive, lax**) toward its former enemies but tried to help them recover and rebuild.

4. As I look over your record, I get the impression that your background in math and science is not (**adequate, ajar**) for an engineering course.

5. For many years Benedict Arnold served his country faithfully, but then he disgraced his name for all time by an (**ajar, infamous**) act of treason.

6. Instead of continuing to (**mull, implore**) over the injustices that people have done to you, forget about the past and concentrate on the future.

7. Our high hopes for an easy victory (**wilted, mulled**) away to nothing as we watched our opponents steadily increase their lead over us.

8. The wonders of nature are as (**innumerable, adequate**) as the grains of sand on a seashore or the leaves on the trees in a forest.

9. Though jaywalking may be considered a(n) (**misdemeanor, overture**), murder is definitely not!

10. As long as the door to compromise is even slightly (**ajar, vindictive**), there is a chance that we will be able to reach an understanding.

11. In spite of all the criticism, our flag still stands throughout the world as a(n) (**pact, emblem**) of justice and freedom.

12. British enlistment posters in World War I assured young men that they would be fighting for "king and country, (**hearth, havoc**) and home."

13. Some parents are quite strict with their children; others are somewhat (**lax, adequate**) and permissive.

14. Instead of resorting at once to armed force, the two nations entered into a diplomatic (**dialogue, havoc**) that eventually resolved the conflict.

15. I was a little miffed when my polite (**stalemates, overtures**) of friendship were so rudely and nastily rejected.

16. The facts of history cannot always be arranged in the form of a smooth and logical (**pact, narrative**).

17. I will not allow our long friendship to be (**marred, implored**) by this unfortunate misunderstanding.

18. The blustery winds on that cold November day played (**havoc, pact**) with my hair all during our sight-seeing tour.

19. The man has such a (**vindictive, gigantic**) ego that absolutely nothing ever seems to fluster, faze, or deflate him.

20. His grim insistence on his "just due" by the terms of our agreement made me think that I'd signed a (**pact, hearth**) with the devil himself!

Unit 12

Definitions   *Note carefully the spelling, pronunciation, and definition of each of the following words. Then write the word in the blank space in the illustrative phrase following.*

1. abound
(ə 'baünd)

(*v.*) to be plentiful, be filled

_____ with ideas

2. braggart
('brag ərt)

(*n.*) a boaster; (*adj.*) boastful in a loud, annoying way

a cocky _____

3. cache
(kash)

(*n.*) a hiding place; something hidden or stored

a _____ of food

4. clarification
(klar ə fə 'kā
shən)

(*n.*) the act of making clear or understandable, an explanation

a _____ of the statement

5. despondent
(di 'spän dənt)

(*adj.*) sad, without hope, discouraged

in a _____ mood

6. embezzle
(em 'bez əl)

(*v.*) to steal property entrusted to one's care

_____ campaign funds

7. heartrending
('härt ren diŋ)

(*adj.*) causing mental pain or grief

a _____ sight

8. leisurely
('lē zhər lē)

(*adj.*) unhurried, taking plenty of time; (*adv.*) in an easygoing or unhurried way

a _____ stroll through the park

9. lethargic
(lə 'thär jik)

(*adj.*) unnaturally sleepy; dull, slow moving; indifferent

became _____ after dinner

10. malady
('mal əd ē)

(*n.*) a sickness, illness, disease, disorder

a childhood _____

11. mellow
('mel ō)

(*adj.*) ripe, well matured; soft, sweet, and rich; gentle, pleasant; (*v.*) to become gentle and sweet

became more _____ with age

12. nomadic
(nō 'ma dik)

(*adj.*) wandering, moving about from place to place

lead a _____ life

13. piecemeal
('pēs mēl)

(*adj.*) one piece at a time; (*adv.*) gradually

do the job _____

14. quest
(kwest)

(*n.*) a search, hunt; (*v.*) to search, seek, ask

the _____ for peace

15. random
('ran dəm)

(*adj.*) by chance, not planned or prearranged; irregular

a _____ sampling of voters

16. rant
(rant)

(v.) to speak wildly and noisily; (n.) loud, violent talk

_____ like a rabble-rouser

17. reinforce
(rē in 'fôrs)

(v.) to make stronger with new materials or support

_____ a building

18. seclusion
(si 'klü zhən)

(n.) isolation from others, solitude

live in _____

19. status
('stā təs)

(n.) a person's condition or position in the eyes of the law; relative rank or standing, especially in society; prestige

boosted her _____

20. turmoil
('tər moil)

(n.) a state of great confusion or disorder; mental strain or agitation

a society in _____

Completing the Sentence

Choose the word from this unit that best completes each of the following sentences. Write the word in the space provided.

1. The two brothers are both fine athletes, but Tom is quiet and modest, while Hal is an awful _____ .

2. Instead of trying to decide which applicants were best suited for the job, he selected two of them at _____ .

3. Arthritis is a(n) _____ that attacks many millions of people, especially in middle and old age.

4. Though I am always full of pep during the morning, I start to become a little _____ as the day wears on.

5. After putting up all week with the noise and confusion of life in the big city, I enjoy the _____ of my mountain retreat on weekends.

6. The park is always full of soapbox orators _____ and raving about the sins of government, society, or the human condition.

7. Apparently the man could pay off his staggering gambling debts only by _____ funds from the company that employed him.

8. The _____ of the French Revolution and the Napoleonic Era was succeeded by 100 years of relative peace and quiet in Europe.

9. Modern-day terrorists are known to secrete sizable _____ of weapons and other essentials in many cities throughout the world.

10. Most detectives solve crimes in a(n) _____ fashion, as clues come to light, rather than all at once.

11. The tenor's voice was rich and _____ , but the baritone's sounded somewhat harsh and unpleasant.

12. The lake so _____ with trout and pickerel that even a person with my limited skill in fishing can catch them easily.

13. Yesterday I read a truly _____ account of the plight of millions of Africans suffering from the effects of a severe famine.

14. When I couldn't at first make out what she wanted me to do, I asked her for some _____ of her instructions.

15. In order to prevent the illegal entry of aliens into the United States, it has been necessary to _____ our border patrols.

16. It's natural to feel a little _____ about not getting the job, but don't let that prevent you from applying for others.

17. Though Ponce de León's _____ for the Fountain of Youth proved futile, he did discover Florida.

18. Hundreds of homeless people now lead essentially _____ lives on the streets of cities all across this country.

19. When I first entered this country, I was classified as a "resident alien," but my _____ has changed since then.

20. Every once in a while, I like to take time out from my busy schedule to have a(n) _____ dinner with old friends.

Synonyms   *Choose the word from this unit that is most nearly **the same** in meaning as each of the following groups of expressions. Write the word on the line given.*

1. roving, roaming, vagrant, migratory, itinerant   _____

2. rank, standing, situation; prestige   _____

3. a search, hunt, pursuit   _____

4. sleepy; lazy, sluggish; indifferent   _____

5. solitude, isolation   _____

6. moving, sad, heartbreaking, poignant   _____

7. chance; haphazard, arbitrary   _____

8. an explanation, elucidation, explication   _____

9. slow, unhurried, relaxed   _____

10. to steal, swindle, defraud   _____

11. sweet, dulcet; gentle; ripe; rich, creamy　———————————

12. to rave, fume, get up on a soapbox　———————————

13. disorder, upheaval, tumult, chaos　———————————

14. a stockpile, hoard, store　———————————

15. dejected, discouraged, down in the dumps　———————————

16. to strengthen, bolster, prop up, support　———————————

17. a boaster, bigmouth, blowhard　———————————

18. bit by bit, a little at a time　———————————

19. an ailment, illness, disease　———————————

20. to burst with, overflow with, teem with　———————————

Antonyms　*Choose the word from this unit that is most nearly* **opposite** *in meaning to each of the following groups of expressions. Write the word on the line given.*

1. peace and quiet, order　———————————

2. wide-awake, alert; energetic, dynamic　———————————

3. all at once, in one fell swoop　———————————

4. jubilant, elated, on top of the world　———————————

5. to lack, want, be in short supply　———————————

6. planned, deliberate; systematic　———————————

7. to weaken, undermine, sap, impair　———————————

8. stationary, settled, rooted, fixed　———————————

9. hasty, hurried, rushed, hectic　———————————

10. amusing, funny, hilarious　———————————

11. unripe, green; harsh, grating, strident　———————————

12. the thick of things　———————————

13. health, well-being　———————————

14. to speak calmly and reasonably; to whisper　———————————

15. someone who doesn't blow his or her own horn　———————————

Choosing the Right Word *Encircle the **boldface** word that more satisfactorily completes each of the following sentences.*

1. The eternal (**quest, seclusion**) for youth and beauty explains the huge sales of cosmetics, to men as well as women.

2. My experience on my summer job has (**reinforced, abounded**) many of the lessons I learned in the classroom.

3. There is a great difference between being quietly confident of your own ability and being an obnoxious (**nomad, braggart**).

4. Though he (**rants, embezzles**) on endlessly about the problems of the world, he has little to offer in the way of solutions to them.

5. As soon as I opened the book, I realized that I had stumbled on a rich (**cache, braggart**) of useful information for my report.

6. People who waste the natural resources of this country are in a sense (**embezzling, reinforcing**) the wealth of future generations.

7. Why would a world-famous writer choose to live in the (**quest, seclusion**) of a country village far from the "madding crowd"?

8. She tried to appear calm and collected, but we could see that her mind was in a state of (**turmoil, status**).

9. Only the fact that they cannot see the seriousness of the emergency can explain their (**lethargic, nomadic**) response to our appeal for help.

10. Instead of such (**mellow, piecemeal**) efforts to prevent air pollution, we need a unified campaign that will be continued for as long as necessary.

11. I believe that education, understanding, and experience provide the only cure for the (**malady, status**) of racial prejudice.

12. Over the years I have learned one thing about rumors: Where the facts are few, fictions (**abound, clarify**).

13. In the (**heartrending, lethargic**) conclusion of the opera, the heroine dies in the arms of her beloved.

14. For weeks a gang of muggers wandered the streets aimlessly, choosing their victims at (**random, piecemeal**) from those who happened by.

15. Our present policy appears to be so contradictory that I believe some (**clarification, turmoil**) of it is in order.

16. At the time when this event happened, I was very angry, but over the years my emotions have (**mellowed, reinforced**).

17. The President went on the air to inform the general public of the present (**malady, status**) of the negotiations with the hijackers.

18. Since I was in no hurry to get where I was going, I decided to set a rather (**random, leisurely**) pace for myself.

19. (**Nomadic, Despondent**) tribes of horse breeders still wander the plains of Central Asia in search of pasturage for their herds.

20. Many doctors believe that when sick people become very (**heartrending, despondent**) about their health, it is more difficult for them to recover.

Review   Units 10–12

Analogies   *In each of the following, encircle the item that best completes the comparison.*

1. knight is to **quest** as
a. nomad is to herd
b. parasite is to meal
c. soldier is to campaign
d. beneficiary is to will

2. farce is to **laughs** as
a. drama is to yawns
b. tragedy is to tears
c. comedy is to sneezes
d. musical is to groans

3. surplus is to **more** as
a. shortage is to less
b. dearth is to more
c. clutter is to less
d. lack is to more

4. overture is to **opera** as
a. plot is to novel
b. dialogue is to play
c. preface is to book
d. index is to dictionary

5. big is to **gigantic** as
a. futile is to random
b. small is to tiny
c. lavish is to adequate
d. ajar is to shut

6. bull is to **bellow** as
a. leopard is to rant
b. elephant is to purr
c. lion is to roar
d. goat is to neigh

7. grueling is to **exhaust** as
a. difficult is to interest
b. knotty is to amaze
c. dull is to bore
d. tiresome is to delight

8. lion is to **den** as
a. tiger is to hearth
b. fox is to cache
c. bear is to seclusion
d. wolf is to lair

9. mar is to **damage** as
a. dismantle is to disassemble
b. shirk is to fulfill
c. implore is to hire
d. reinforce is to undermine

10. hearth is to **fire** as
a. sink is to soap
b. well is to water
c. bucket is to handle
d. floor is to dirt

11. braggart is to **boast** as
a. showoff is to strut
b. pickpocket is to botch
c. daredevil is to wilt
d. spoilsport is to mull

12. lethargic is to **energy** as
a. mellow is to richness
b. heartrending is to pity
c. lavish is to size
d. leisurely is to speed

13. despondent is to **cheer** as
a. morbid is to gloom
b. timid is to courage
c. confident is to clarification
d. hospitable is to courtesy

14. malady is to **sick** as
a. injury is to hurt
b. turmoil is to calm
c. status is to worried
d. problem is to content

15. vindictive is to **revenge** as
a. greedy is to success
b. lazy is to fame
c. envious is to knowledge
d. grasping is to gain

16. narrative is to **told** as
a. dialogue is to thought
b. symphony is to played
c. overture is to sung
d. pact is to spoken

17. cache is to **hidden** as
a. stalemate is to won
b. turmoil is to given
c. loot is to stolen
d. misdemeanor is to forgotten

18. embezzler is to **swindle** as
a. dictator is to pamper
b. coward is to veto
c. judge is to mar
d. beggar is to implore

Synonyms   In each of the following groups, encircle the word or expression that is most nearly **the same** in meaning as the **boldface word** in the introductory phrase.

1. the **quest** for world peace
a. reason   b. search   c. support   d. desire

2. bellow a command
a. receive   b. disobey   c. hear   d. shout

3. a **clarification** of your remarks
a. knowledge   b. explanation   c. summary   d. report

4. a **mellow** tone
a. angry   b. strange   c. rich   d. harsh

5. surplus material
a. needed   b. extra   c. flimsy   d. expensive

6. nomadic tribes
a. warlike   b. settled   c. roving   d. peaceful

7. with the window **ajar**
a. stuck   b. partly open   c. broken   d. clean

8. an **adequate** supply of water
a. sufficient   b. abundant   c. scant   d. fresh

9. a **lavish** gift
a. extravagant   b. cheap   c. new   d. funny

10. the **emblem** of peace
a. result   b. symbol   c. lack   d. cause

11. create **havoc**
a. work   b. confusion   c. interest   d. prosperity

12. clutter the shelves
a. build   b. arrange   c. label   d. litter

13. got the information **piecemeal**
a. little by little   b. accurately   c. unwillingly   d. quickly

14. rant and rave
a. write   b. talk wildly   c. lie   d. joke

15. mulled over their suggestions
a. ignored   b. accepted   c. criticized   d. pondered

16. dilapidated furniture
a. brand new   b. antique   c. run-down   d. modern

Shades of Meaning   Read each sentence carefully. Then encircle the item that best completes the statement below the sentence.

Edgar Allan Poe's story "The Black Cat" ends with the discovery of the cache in which the narrator has walled up the animal he has slain. **(2)**

1. In line 2 the word **cache** is used to mean
a. hiding place   b. grave   c. hoard   d. buried coffin

Am I guilty of "conspicuous consumption" if I purchase something solely for the status it is supposed to lend me? **(2)**

2. The word **status** in line 2 is best defined as
a. fame
b. prestige
c. condition
d. position

Her lax smile told me that she had not found the vocabulary test as difficult as she had feared. **(2)**

3. In line 1 the word **lax** most nearly means
a. undisciplined
b. negligent
c. relaxed
d. sarcastic

As the park rangers approached the carcass left behind by poachers, a few jackals went shirking into the brush. **(2)**

4. In line 2 the word **shirking** is used to mean
a. neglecting
b. avoiding
c. sidestepping
d. sneaking

The last words of the 16th-century French author François Rabelais are reported to have been "Draw the curtain; the farce is played." **(2)**

5. The best definition for the word **farce** in line 2 is
a. sham
b. comedy
c. humor
d. melodrama

Antonyms   *In each of the following groups, encircle the word or expression that is most nearly **opposite** in meaning to the **boldface word** in the introductory phrase.*

1. a **lethargic** mood
a. dreamy   b. agreeable   c. nasty   d. energetic

2. a **gigantic** dog
a. shaggy   b. tiny   c. fierce   d. new

3. when the flower **wilted**
a. faded   b. spoiled   c. died   d. bloomed

4. a very **grueling** race
a. easy   b. tiring   c. long   d. interesting

5. **veto** the plan
a. forbid   b. cancel   c. approve   d. suggest

6. to **reinforce** the beams
a. paint   b. construct   c. test   d. weaken

7. **shirk** one's duty
a. describe   b. ignore   c. understand   d. do

8. a **futile** effort
a. large   b. tiring   c. successful   d. new

9. **implore** mercy
a. demand   b. beg   c. love   d. defend

10. dismantle the bomb
a. explode   b. assemble   c. design   d. destroy

11. left the house in **turmoil**
a. flames   b. haste   c. secrecy   d. peace

12. worked in a **leisurely** way
a. well-organized   b. easygoing   c. hasty   d. artistic

13. a **heartrending** story
a. funny   b. sad   c. modern   d. typical

14. in a **despondent** mood
a. jubilant   b. gloomy   c. unusual   d. sour

15. inclined to **pamper** the children
a. mistreat   b. educate   c. coddle   d. adopt

Completing the Sentence

From the following lists of words, choose the one that best completes each of the sentences below. Write the word in the space provided.

Group A

emblem	mellow	adequate	beneficiary
farce	lair	mull	reinforce
lax	futile	overture	mar

1. On that tiny island in the Caribbean Sea the pirates had set up their secret _____ , where they stored all their treasure.

2. Before the curtain goes up on Act One, the orchestra plays the composer's most famous _____ .

3. As the master violinist drew her bow across her instrument, the gloriously _____ tones filled the concert hall.

4. When I told my father that I had gone out for basketball, he was so proud that it _____ my determination to make the team.

5. On the back of a dollar bill, you will see a(n) _____ that shows an eagle and the motto *E Pluribus Unum.*

Group B

random	abound	dialogue	veto
despondent	clarification	seclusion	hearth
piecemeal	lavish	pact	havoc

1. If our _____ is to work out successfully, all the terms must be clearly stated and fully understood by both sides.

2. The fire in the _____ burned low as we waited anxiously for the safe return of the children.

3. I want to be popular, but I'm not going to become _____ just because a few people don't like me.

4. After the death of his wife, he seemed to lose interest in other people and chose to live in almost total _____ .

5. The play would be more effective if the _____ were written so that it sounded like the speech of real people.

Word Families

A. *On the line provided, write a **noun form** of each of the following words.*

EXAMPLE: dilapidated — **dilapidation**

1. futile _____

2. adequate _____

3. lax _____

4. vindictive _____

5. mellow _____

6. despondent _____

7. hospitable _____

8. lavish _____

9. leisurely _____

10. notorious _____

11. abound _____

12. morbid _____

13. reinforce _____

14. embezzle _____

15. lethargic _____

16. nomadic _____

17. random _____

18. dismantle _____

19. infamous _____

20. shirk _____

B. *On the line provided, write a **verb** related to each of the following words.*

EXAMPLE: dilapidated — **dilapidate**

1. clarification _____

2. braggart   _____

3. narrative   _____

4. seclusion   _____

5. misdemeanor   _____

6. timidity   _____

Filling the Blanks   _Encircle the pair of words that best complete the meaning of each of the following passages._

1. Since the soil is so remarkably rich and fertile, various kinds of crops can be grown in _____ . The farmers keep what they need for themselves and sell off the _____ at a handsome profit.

  a. abundance . . . surplus   c. lavishness . . . hospitality
  b. seclusion . . . reinforcements   d. leisure . . . adequacy

2. The earliest inhabitants of North America lived _____ lives. They were constantly on the move in pursuit of the game that made up the greater part of their diet. This endless _____ for food eventually took them to all parts of the continent.

  a. nomadic . . . quest   c. pampered . . . malady
  b. grueling . . . cache   d. lethargic . . . status

3. As he sat by the fire that glowed in the _____ , the old sailor entertained the children with a(n) _____ of his adventures on the high seas, beginning when he was a boy of twelve almost sixty years before.

  a. lair . . . farce   c. hearth . . . narrative
  b. cache . . . dialogue   d. clutter . . . overture

4. Before we can even think about renovating this _____ old house, we must remove all the worthless _____ that is strewn around the rooms and blocking the entrances.

  a. gigantic . . . cache   c. mellow . . . havoc
  b. dilapidated . . . clutter   d. futile . . . surplus

5. "I am still _____ the matter over in my mind," the President told the press. "When I have reached a decision, I will either sign the bill or _____ it."

  a. mellowing . . . botch   c. mulling . . . veto
  b. narrating . . . dismantle   d. clarifying . . . mar

Analogies   *In each of the following, encircle the item that best completes the comparison.*

1. alliance is to **pact** as
a. truce is to cease-fire
b. dynasty is to brawl
c. anecdote is to oration
d. regime is to onslaught

2. ratify is to **veto** as
a. mar is to disfigure
b. fluster is to bewilder
c. procure is to ordain
d. renovate is to dilapidate

3. innumerable is to **count** as
a. indispensable is to employ
b. interminable is to begin
c. illegible is to read
d. inflammable is to kindle

4. implore is to **entreat** as
a. interrogate is to question
b. parch is to quench
c. accelerate is to decrease
d. nurture is to stifle

5. puny is to **gigantic** as
a. foremost is to prominent
b. lethargic is to dynamic
c. grueling is to graphic
d. vicious is to malignant

6. fruitless is to **futile** as
a. spirited is to animated
b. rural is to urban
c. orthodox is to quaint
d. amiss is to upright

7. reinforce is to **more** as
a. flourish is to less
b. shirk is to more
c. erode is to less
d. eradicate is to more

8. despondent is to **melancholy** as
a. indifferent is to enthusiasm
b. peevish is to courtesy
c. sullen is to joy
d. indignant is to wrath

9. jaywalking is to **misdemeanor** as
a. forgery is to vice
b. homicide is to felony
c. embezzlement is to blunder
d. perjury is to error

10. buffoon is to **farce** as
a. doctor is to patient
b. farmer is to plow
c. acrobat is to circus
d. bystander is to accident

Shades of Meaning   *Read each sentence carefully. Then encircle the item that best completes the statement below the sentence.*

The current was swift in the shallows along the bank, but once we paddled into deeper water, the river turned quite sullen. **(2)**

1. The word **sullen** in line 2 is used to mean
   a. silent   b. sluggish   c. morose   d. surly

It was the custom in many homes in Victorian America to serve mulled beverages to guests at holiday time. **(2)**

2. The best definition for the word **mulled** in line 1 is
   a. pondered   c. heated and flavored
   b. chilled and diluted   d. homemade

One side of the packing material was molded to form a pattern of tiny plastic nubs to absorb shock. **(2)**

3. In line 2 the word **nubs** most nearly means
   a. cores   b. cruxes   c. hearts   d. knobs

The story was so predictable and the characters so dull that it's no wonder
the show met such a lethargic response.   (2)

4. The word **lethargic** in line 2 is best defined as
  a. indifferent   c. enthusiastic
  b. lazy   d. critical

The death of Stonewall Jackson in 1863 left a void in the ranks of Lee's
generals that no other officer was able to fill.   (2)

5. In line 1 the word **void** is used to mean
  a. annulment   c. vacancy
  b. cancellation   d. promotion

**Filling
the Blanks**
*Encircle the pair of words that best complete the
meaning of each of the following passages.*

1. "Staircases and hallways that are _____ with all kinds of

junk constitute a real fire _____ ," the fire marshal told us

when he inspected our plant recently.
  a. disrupted . . . ingredient   c. cluttered . . . hazard
  b. inflicted . . . momentum   d. retarded . . . stalemate

2. The hunters set various kinds of traps to _____ the beast

when it left its mountain lair in _____ of food and water for

its young.
  a. goad . . . uncertainty   c. plague . . . vengeance
  b. snare . . . quest   d. frustrate . . . foretaste

3. Though modern medicine can _____ remedies for many of

the _____ that afflict us, it still hasn't found a surefire cure

for cancer.
  a. prescribe . . . maladies   c. ordain . . . narratives
  b. verify . . . remnants   d. presume . . . surpluses

4. During the African dry season the land becomes so _____

that even a mighty river can be reduced to a mere _____ .
  a. sodden . . . résumé   c. lubricated . . . iota
  b. wilted . . . nub   d. parched . . . trickle

5. The sudden wail of the air-raid siren and the ominous _____

of airplanes overhead sent dozens of civilians _____ for

cover.
  a. luster . . . floundering   c. rant . . . yearning
  b. drone . . . scurrying   d. brood . . . hurtling

Unit 13

Definitions

Note carefully the spelling, pronunciation, and definition of each of the following words. Then write the word in the blank space in the illustrative phrase following.

1. **agitation**
   (aj i 'tā shən)

   (*n.*) a violent stirring or movement; noisy confusion, excitement; a stirring up of public enthusiasm

   _____ for tax reform

2. **blurt**
   (blərt)

   (*v.*) to say suddenly or without thinking

   _____ out the truth

3. **chronological**
   (krän əl 'äj i kəl)

   (*adj.*) arranged in order of time of occurrence

   in _____ order

4. **countenance**
   ('kaún tə nəns)

   (*n.*) a face, facial expression; (*v.*) to tolerate or approve

   her smiling _____

5. **diminish**
   (di 'min ish)

   (*v.*) to make or become smaller, reduce in size

   _____ in popularity

6. **enchant**
   (en 'chant)

   (*v.*) to please greatly; to charm, put under a magic spell

   _____ everyone in the room

7. **fluctuate**
   ('flək chü āt)

   (*v.*) to change continually; to move up and down

   prices that _____

8. **foster**
   ('fôs tər)

   (*v.*) to bring up, give care to; to promote, encourage; (*adj.*) in the same family but not related by birth

   a _____ child

9. **grovel**
   ('gräv əl)

   (*v.*) to humble oneself, act in a fearful and servile way; to lie face downward; to indulge in something base or unworthy

   _____ in the dirt

10. **handicraft**
    ('han dē kraft)

    (*n.*) work done by hand; a trade requiring hand skill; (*adj.*) relating to skilled work done by hand

    a _____ shop

11. **hilarious**
    (hi 'lâr ē əs)

    (*adj.*) extremely funny, causing loud amusement

    a _____ story

12. **ignite**
    (ig 'nīt)

    (*v.*) to set on fire, cause to burn; to heat up, excite

    _____ the charcoal

13. **magnitude**
    ('mag nə tüd)

    (*n.*) the great size or importance of something

    the _____ of the task

14. **massive**
    ('mas iv)

    (*adj.*) large and heavy; great in size or scope

    a _____ block of stone

15. maternal
(mə 'tər nəl)

(*adj.*) of or like a mother

_____ responsibilities

16. pall
(pôl)

(*v.*) to lose in interest, attraction, or effectiveness; to become tiresome; (*n.*) a dark covering, something that conceals

cast a _____ over the proceedings

17. reputable
('rep yət ə bəl)

(*adj.*) well thought of, having a good reputation

a _____ dealer

18. revere
(ri 'vēr)

(*v.*) to love and respect deeply, honor greatly

_____ our flag

19. saga
('säg ə)

(*n.*) a narrative of heroic exploits; a long, detailed account

an Icelandic _____

20. stodgy
('stäj ē)

(*adj.*) dull, boring; old-fashioned, hidebound; lumpy, thick

a _____ person

Completing the Sentence

Choose the word from this unit that best completes each of the following sentences. Write the word in the space provided.

1. Our study of American history has taught us to _____ the great men and women who founded this nation.

2. Statements _____ out in anger may often be regretted for a long time afterward.

3. We had hoped to have a wonderful time at the party, but the sad news of Anne's accident cast a(n) _____ over the gathering.

4. We will donate the proceeds of the cake sale to any _____ charity you may select.

5. His attitudes are so incredibly _____ and hidebound that they would have been considered old-fashioned 100 years ago!

6. In the _____ *of Eric the Red*, there is a very interesting account of the Norse discovery of North America in A.D. 1000.

7. Can you imagine my _____ when I was told I would have to take over the lead role in the play immediately, with no rehearsals!

8. "When I was living among the Stone Age aborigines of Western Australia, I learned many curious skills and _____ ," the explorer said.

9. The number and the _____ of the problems faced by the President of the United States are almost beyond our imagination.

10. The two little girls playing "house" down in the basement fussed over the doll with all the _____ care and attention that their own mothers bestowed on them.

11. How can you _____ such rude behavior in a young child!

12. Even though I need a job badly, I still have my self-respect, and I am not going to _____ just to get work.

13. With no money coming in and my daily expenses continuing to mount, my savings have _____ at an alarming rate.

14. The pilot light of the stove will automatically _____ the burner when the handle is turned to the "on" position.

15. The audience was _____ not only by the lovely voice of the soprano but by her youthful good looks as well.

16. She was very fortunate to have talented and sympathetic teachers who _____ her career.

17. The _____ towers of the World Trade Center rising more than 100 stories above us made us feel like ants.

18. Instead of moving steadily upwards or steadily downwards, the price of the stock I own has been _____ all year.

19. The waves of laughter from the audience indicated that those around me found the comedian's jokes _____ , but I was bored silly.

20. Educators report that there is often a vast difference between a child's mental age and his or her _____ age.

Synonyms *Choose the word from this unit that is most nearly **the same** in meaning as each of the following groups of expressions. Write the word on the line given.*

1. reliable, respectable, trustworthy _____

2. a manual art, manual skill; handiwork _____

3. to honor, admire, esteem, cherish _____

4. stuffy, hidebound; dull, boring _____

5. to promote, support, nurture _____

6. to inflame, light, kindle _____

7. bulky, huge, immense, monumental _____

8. gloom, a shadow; to bore, weary _____

9. a face; an expression; to tolerate   _____

10. motherly; protective, sympathetic   _____

11. to blab out, let slip   _____

12. size, extent, importance, immensity   _____

13. to lessen, reduce, decrease, dwindle   _____

14. to waver, seesaw, oscillate   _____

15. in sequence of time, consecutive   _____

16. to delight, thrill; to bewitch   _____

17. to crouch, cower, cringe; to wallow   _____

18. excitement, disquiet, uneasiness, upset   _____

19. very funny, highly amusing   _____

20. a heroic tale, epic, chronicle   _____

Antonyms   *Choose the word from this unit that is most nearly* ***opposite*** *in meaning to each of the following groups of expressions. Write the word on the line given.*

1. to scorn, disdain; to mock, deride   _____

2. smallness, unimportance, insignificance   _____

3. boring, dull; humorless; heartrending   _____

4. to bore; to nauseate, disgust   _____

5. fatherly, paternal   _____

6. to quench, extinguish, douse, put out   _____

7. to stay put, remain unchanged   _____

8. to increase, enlarge, augment   _____

9. peace of mind, composure, calm   _____

10. shady, unsavory, questionable   _____

11. flimsy, frail, thin   _____

12. forward-looking, avant-garde, progressive   _____

13. to disapprove of, not to stand for   _____

14. light, brightness; to intrigue, fascinate   _____

15. to stifle, smother, quash, discourage   _____

Choosing the Right Word   *Encircle the **boldface** word that more satisfactorily completes each of the following sentences.*

1. Many professional and executive people today have made enjoyable hobbies of such (**handicrafts, sagas**) as carpentry and weaving.

2. The speaker alarmed us when he said that our whole system of handling lawbreakers has (**massive, stodgy**) faults that will be difficult to correct.

3. For more than a hundred years, the delightful adventures of Alice in Wonderland have been (**enchanting, palling**) readers young and old.

4. In my excitement, I accidentally (**blurted, agitated**) out the very thing that I was trying so hard to conceal.

5. For a long time my favorite TV entertainment was police and detective programs, but now they are beginning to (**pall, enchant**).

6. Any editorial about pollution appearing in such a (**maternal, reputable**) newspaper is bound to make a strong impression on many citizens.

7. The cowboy on his trusty quarter horse plays a prominent part in the (**saga, magnitude**) of the Old West.

8. Though there has of late been a good deal of (**countenance, agitation**) for reform in this area, nothing much has come of it so far.

9. The mood at the party was so (**massive, hilarious**) that everyone was laughing even when nothing particularly funny was going on.

10. The man was such a controversial figure in his own time that he was both (**fostered, revered**) as a saint and despised as an impostor.

11. Many older people complain that the warm spirit of neighborliness has greatly (**diminished, revered**) under the conditions of city living.

12. Like everyone else, I want to be well liked, but I will not (**grovel, fluctuate**) before public opinion when I am firmly convinced that it is wrong.

13. If it were not for the strong (**maternal, hilarious**) instinct to protect the young, many species of animals could not survive.

14. One of the sure signs of a country that is not free is that the people in power will not (**countenance, blurt**) any criticism of their acts.

15. As the game went on, and the lead continued to change hands, our feelings (**fostered, fluctuated**) from joy to despair and back again.

16. The Tea Act of 1773 was one of the sparks that helped (**ignite, enchant**) the American Revolution.

17. When the Wright brothers made the first successful airplane flight, few people realized the (**pall, magnitude**) of their achievement.

18. My love of reading, (**fostered, diminished**) by my parents since early childhood, has continued to grow through the years.

19. So many different battles took place during the Civil War that I often have difficulty remembering the correct (**chronology, handicraft**).

20. Her charming personality and sparkling wit brought a breath of fresh air into the (**stodgy, hilarious**) atmosphere of our stuffy old club.

Unit 14

Definitions

Note carefully the spelling, pronunciation, and definition of each of the following words. Then write the word in the blank space in the illustrative phrase following.

1. **affliction**
(ə 'flik shən)

(*n.*) a physical ailment; a cause of pain or trouble, misfortune

an _____ of the elderly

2. **akin**
(ə 'kin)

(*adj.*) related by blood; having similar qualities or character

ideas _____ to ours

3. **cosmopolitan**
(käz mə 'päl ə tən)

(*adj.*) found in most parts of the world; having many fields of interest; of worldwide scope; sophisticated

a _____ point of view

4. **elongate**
(i 'lôŋ gāt)

(*v.*) to grow in length, become longer; to extend the length of

_____ an antenna

5. **gala**
('gā lə)

(*n.*) a public entertainment marking a special event, a festive occasion; (*adj.*) festive, showy

a _____ performance

6. **gaudy**
('gô dē)

(*adj.*) flashy, showy; not in good taste

a _____ outfit

7. **gratitude**
('grat ə tüd)

(*n.*) appreciation, thankfulness

express one's _____

8. **heed**
(hēd)

(*v.*) to pay careful attention to, notice; to be guided by; (*n.*) close attention or consideration

_____ their advice

9. **hoax**
(hōks)

(*n.*) an act intended to trick or deceive, a fraud; (*v.*) to trick, deceive

a literary _____

10. **impartial**
(im 'pär shəl)

(*adj.*) just, unbiased, fair, not taking sides

an _____ judge

11. **impostor**
(im 'päs tər)

(*n.*) a swindler, deceiver; one who uses a false name or character in order to cheat

expose the _____

12. **inflate**
(in 'flāt)

(*v.*) to fill with air or gas; to swell or puff out; to make something appear larger than it is

_____ the balloon

13. **meager**
('mē gər)

(*adj.*) poor, scant, unsatisfactory; thin, slight

a _____ allowance

14. meditate
('med ə tāt)

(v.) to think about deeply and quietly, reflect upon; to plan, intend

_____ on the meaning of life

15. nutritious
(nü 'trish əs)

(adj.) nourishing, valuable and satisfying as food

a _____ meal

16. oppress
(ə 'pres)

(v.) to govern or rule cruelly or unjustly; to weigh heavily upon

_____ the people

17. pedestrian
(pə 'des trē ən)

(n.) one who goes on foot; (adj.) relating to walking; on foot; ordinary, dull, unimaginative

_____ traffic

18. transmit
(tranz 'mit)

(v.) to send on, pass along, send out

_____ a message

19. vanquish
('vaŋ kwish)

(v.) to defeat in a battle or contest, overthrow; to overcome a feeling or condition

_____ one's enemies

20. wan
(wän)

(adj.) unnaturally pale or sickly-looking; lacking vitality; dim, faint; weak, ineffectual

a _____ complexion

Completing the Sentence

Choose the word from this unit that best completes each of the following sentences. Write the word in the space provided.

1. With a population made up of people from many different lands, New York City is one of the most _____ places in the world.

2. Modern technology has provided us with the computer, a truly marvelous device for collecting, sorting, and _____ information quickly.

3. An earthworm moves by first _____ and then contracting its wonderfully elastic body.

4. After beating off the enemy's initial assault, our brave troops delivered a series of crippling counterattacks that _____ the foe.

5. If you had only _____ my warnings, all this trouble could easily have been avoided.

6. Most of us are so busy with everyday concerns that we can find little or no time to _____ on the larger issues of life.

7. Most cities have now passed laws to discourage _____ from crossing against the light or jaywalking.

8. Since I am a very close friend of his, you cannot expect me to be totally

_____ in judging your criticisms of him.

9. I don't expect you to throw yourself on your knees, but I wish you'd show a

little _____ for the things I've done for you.

10. The big clown's _____ costume was in sharp contrast to the simple white outfits worn by the trapeze artists.

11. Modern medical science can do wonders for people suffering from various

physical or emotional _____ .

12. Refusing to be _____ by unjust laws, the American colonists rose in revolt against the British government.

13. The distraught mother's _____ smile and worried expression reflected her sense of anxiety over her lost child.

14. Superstars and other celebrities are usually very much in evidence at such

_____ events as opening night of a new Broadway show.

15. Have you ever tried to _____ a bicycle tire with one of those old-fashioned hand pumps?

16. "Junk food" may look attractive and taste great, but it is by no means as

_____ as much plainer fare.

17. Unfortunately, the region cannot support a very large population because

its natural resources are so _____ .

18. Though the newspapers hailed the find as the "discovery of the century," it

turned out to be nothing but an outrageous _____ .

19. "Although these two words are not related etymologically," the professor

observed, "they are _____ to each other in meaning."

20. The family lawyer proved that the young man claiming to be the missing

heir was no more than a(n) _____ .

Synonyms *Choose the word from this unit that is most nearly **the same** in meaning as each of the following groups of expressions. Write the word on the line given.*

1. to pass on, convey, relay, deliver _____

2. to blow up, pump up; to enlarge, exaggerate _____

3. someone on foot; commonplace, prosaic _____

4. to defeat, beat, conquer, subdue _____

5. to mistreat, persecute, grind underfoot _____

6. just, fair, unbiased, disinterested

7. nourishing, healthful, wholesome

8. a deception, ruse, fake; to dupe

9. ashen, pasty, pallid, bloodless; sickly, gaunt

10. related, kindred, similar

11. to pay attention to, listen to

12. flashy, garish, loud, vulgar

13. to ponder, contemplate, muse, ruminate

14. slight, scanty, skimpy, sparse

15. a woe, misfortune; torment, anguish

16. thankfulness, appreciation

17. global, international; sophisticated

18. a cheat, swindler, trickster, four-flusher

19. to lengthen, stretch, protract, extend

20. an extravaganza, fête; spectacular, grand

Antonyms   *Choose the word from this unit that is most nearly* ***opposite*** *in meaning to each of the following groups of expressions. Write the word on the line given.*

1. unrelated, dissimilar

2. a driver, rider; original, novel

3. to pay no attention to, ignore

4. to shorten, abbreviate, contract, curtail

5. one-sided, prejudiced, biased, partial

6. narrow, unsophisticated, provincial

7. ample, plentiful, abundant, lavish

8. to be defeated by, succumb to

9. to deflate, flatten; to diminish

10. restrained, quiet, sober, sedate, tasteful

11. a blessing, boon; a joy

12. rosy, ruddy, blooming, radiant

13. to pamper, coddle; to free, liberate

Choosing the Right Word

*Encircle the **boldface** word that more satisfactorily completes each of the following sentences.*

1. We are so accustomed to TV that we tend to forget how wonderful it is to (**oppress, transmit**) colored images from one place to another.

2. The speaker had important things to say, but his way of expressing himself was so dull and (**nutritious, pedestrian**) that he lost our interest.

3. Try as he might, the sideshow barker couldn't convince me that the "real live mermaid" inside the tent wasn't just a clever (**hoax, gala**).

4. Such extravaganzas as the "Night of 100 Stars" are usually designed to be (**gala, wan**) charity benefits for worthy causes.

5. Is there any country in the world in which the terrible (**affliction, impostor**) of poverty has been entirely overcome?

6. By continuing to praise his extremely modest accomplishments, you are helping to (**inflate, transmit**) his already oversized ego.

7. Education and compassion are the only weapons by which we will (**heed, vanquish**) prejudice and superstition once and for all.

8. After a lifetime of travel in dozens of countries all over the world, she is highly (**cosmopolitan, akin**) in her tastes and ideas.

9. Shakespeare's advice about dressing— "rich, not (**gaudy, akin**)"—still holds true in today's world.

10. Have you ever noticed that as the sun sinks lower in the sky, shadows become (**elongated, cosmopolitan**)?

11. A "viewing diet" made up entirely of game shows may be entertaining, but it is not particularly (**meager, nutritious**), mentally speaking.

12. The man's pathetically (**wan, elongated**) personality is matched only by the hopelessly bland and lifeless statements that issue from his mouth.

13. My mind and body were so (**oppressed, heeded**) by the stifling heat that afternoon that I couldn't do anything at all.

14. I'd describe nostalgia as a feeling more (**meager, akin**) to yearning than to grief.

15. We won the game because we kept our heads and paid no (**gratitude, heed**) to the insulting remarks made by our opponents.

16. When she came out on the stage, she was greeted by a (**meager, gaudy**) round of applause; before she left, she had the audience cheering.

17. He claimed to be a famous multimillionaire, but when he tried to borrow bus fare, we realized he was a(n) (**pedestrian, impostor**).

18. Is it necessary for you to go into the woods to (**meditate, inflate**) every time you have to make a routine decision?

19. Each scholarship candidate was identified by a number, so that the people doing the grading would be absolutely (**impartial, pedestrian**).

20. Mere words cannot express our (**affliction, gratitude**) for your splendid services to our school.

Unit 15

Definitions

Note carefully the spelling, pronunciation, and definition of each of the following words. Then write the word in the blank space in the illustrative phrase following.

1. authoritative
(ə 'thär ə tā tiv)

(*adj.*) official, coming from a source that calls for obedience or belief; dictatorial

an _____ source

2. bankrupt
('baŋk rəpt)

(*adj.*) in a state of financial ruin; (*v.*) to ruin financially; (*n.*) one who has been ruined financially

a _____ company

3. clamor
('klam ər)

(*n.*) a public outcry; any loud and continued noise; (*v.*) to call for by loud, continued outcries

_____ for reform

4. coincide
(kō in 'sīd)

(*v.*) to be in full agreement; to be the same in nature, character, or function; to happen at the same time

beliefs that _____ with ours

5. cynical
('sin ə kəl)

(*adj.*) inclined to believe the worst of people; bitterly mocking or sneering

a _____ attitude

6. despot
('des pət)

(*n.*) a ruler who oppresses his or her subjects, a tyrant

a _____ like Nero

7. feud
(fyüd)

(*n.*) a bitter, long-term quarrel; (*v.*) to fight or quarrel with

a senseless _____

8. haggle
('hag əl)

(*v.*) to argue in a petty way, especially about a price

_____ over details

9. hardy
('här dē)

(*adj.*) able to bear up under difficult conditions or harsh treatment; brave and tough

a _____ variety of plant

10. harmonious
(här 'mō nē əs)

(*adj.*) able to get along together well; combining different elements that blend pleasingly; melodious

a _____ group

11. hoard
(hôrd)

(*v.*) to store up, save; (*n.*) a hidden store or supply

_____ money

12. indisposed
(in dis 'pōzd)

(*adj., part.*) slightly ill; disinclined to do something

_____ with a cold

13. legacy
('leg ə sē)

(*n.*) an inheritance; something handed down from an ancestor or from the past

a rich _____ of knowledge

14. legitimate
(lə ′jit ə mət)

(*adj.*) lawful, rightful; reasonable, justifiable

a _____ criticism

15. mirth
(mərth)

(*n.*) merry fun, gaiety; laughter

filled with _____

16. officiate
(ə ′fish ē āt)

(*v.*) to perform the duties of an office; to conduct a religious ceremony; to referee

_____ at the service

17. partial
(′pär shəl)

(*adj.*) not complete; favoring one side over another; showing a strong liking for someone or something

_____ to sweets

18. patronize
(′pā trə nīz)

(*v.*) to give one's business to regularly as a customer; to support, provide financial help; to treat someone as an inferior while making a show of being kind or gracious

_____ the local stores

19. rite
(rīt)

(*n.*) a ceremony; the customary form of a ceremony; any formal custom or practice

the marriage _____

20. sagacious
(sə ′gā shəs)

(*adj.*) shrewd; wise in a keen, practical way

a _____ leader

Completing the Sentence

Choose the word from this unit that best completes each of the following sentences. Write the word in the space provided.

1. Although she had no previous experience as a treasurer, she showed herself to be highly _____ in the way she handled money.

2. Since your program for cleaning up the lakefront _____ with ours, why can't we work together?

3. My aunt called to say that she would not be able to visit us because she was _____ with an attack of hay fever.

4. I think your price for the tennis racket is too high, but since I'm in no mood to _____ with you, I'll take it.

5. When you say that "everyone is out to take advantage of everyone else," I think you're being much too _____ .

6. I like a good laugh as much as anyone, but I realized that such a solemn ceremony was not the time for _____ .

7. Is it true that squirrels _____ nuts and other foods that they can use over the winter?

8. Our supervisor became extremely unpopular with us because he acted like a(n) _____ toward everyone in the department.

9. True, business has been poor, but we are covering our expenses and can assure you that there's no danger of our going _____ .

10. The students were urged to _____ the local merchants who advertised in the school paper.

11. The referee who _____ at a hockey game must have the stamina to keep up with the players and the patience to put up with them.

12. The fact that the baseball season is opening today is certainly not a(n) _____ excuse for being absent from school.

13. Where can I get a(n) _____ estimate of how the population of the United States is likely to change in the years ahead?

14. Nothing will be accomplished unless the members of the committee work together in a(n) _____ fashion.

15. The pagan religions of ancient times revolved around the performance of various _____ designed to ensure the fertility of the land.

16. About five minutes before feeding time, all the babies in the nursery start to _____ for their bottles.

17. The pioneers who settled the West were _____ people who could cope with difficulties and dangers of all kinds.

18. Historians are still examining the deadly _____ that arose between the Hatfield and McCoy families more than 100 years ago.

19. We must be prepared to defend the _____ of freedom that we have inherited from earlier generations of Americans.

20. I am making only a(n) _____ payment at the present time and will pay off the balance in installments.

Synonyms   *Choose the word from this unit that is most nearly **the same** in meaning as each of the following groups of expressions. Write the word on the line given.*

1. smart, wise, clever, astute, shrewd   _____

2. incomplete; biased, prejudiced; fond of   _____

3. melodious, tuneful; agreeable, compatible   _____

4. a ceremony, observance, ritual, liturgy   _____

5. reliable, official; authoritarian   _____

6. to bargain with, dicker with, wrangle   _____

7. to chair, preside, emcee, moderate _____

8. flat broke, insolvent _____

9. ailing, unwell; disinclined, reluctant _____

10. rugged, sturdy; resolute, stalwart _____

11. lawful, legal; right, proper; genuine _____

12. merriment, laughter, glee _____

13. to do business with, deal with, trade with _____

14. a dispute, quarrel, vendetta _____

15. a store, stockpile, cache; to amass _____

16. to agree, concur; to happen together _____

17. an inheritance, bequest; a heritage _____

18. an uproar, din, racket; to cry out for _____

19. a dictator, tyrant, autocrat _____

20. skeptical, sarcastic, contemptuous _____

Antonyms   *Choose the word from this unit that is most nearly* **opposite** *in meaning to each of the following groups of expressions. Write the word on the line given.*

1. to waste, throw away, squander _____

2. gloom, sadness, sorrow _____

3. unlawful, illegal; improper; unauthorized _____

4. frail, feeble, weak _____

5. a pact, agreement; harmony, concord _____

6. unofficial, unreliable _____

7. silly, foolish, ill-advised, dopey _____

8. to boycott, refuse to deal with _____

9. healthy; willing, eager _____

10. financially sound, solvent _____

11. hopeful, optimistic _____

12. complete; fair, just, unbiased _____

13. harsh, grating; discordant _____

114

Choosing the   *Encircle the **boldface** word that more satisfactorily*
Right Word   *completes each of the following sentences.*

1. A good sports official pays no attention to the (**clamor, mirth**) of the crowd when a decision goes against the home team.

2. We cannot accept the idea that capital and labor must constantly (**feud, coincide**) with each other.

3. I am annoyed by the (**haggling, patronizing**) way in which they keep reminding me "how a well-bred person behaves."

4. The jury was impressed by the fact that the testimony of two witnesses who were complete strangers (**coincided, clamored**) in every detail.

5. She may give the impression of being a simple old woman, but we have found her to be unusually (**sagacious, indisposed**) in judging people.

6. I was (**hardy, indisposed**) to accept the halfhearted invitation that reached me only a day before the party.

7. Why (**haggle, officiate**) over minor details when we are in agreement on the main issue?

8. If you're looking for a witty, charming personality to (**officiate, coincide**) at the awards dinner, need I say that I'm available?

9. The (**harmonious, authoritative**) tone in which she gave the order left no doubt in anyone's mind that she expected full obedience.

10. Graduating from high school, marriage, and the birth of one's first child are all part of the (**rites, hoards**) of passage from a teenager to an adult.

11. In the period ahead there may be shortages of some foodstuffs, but we will only make things worse if we resort to (**patronizing, hoarding**).

12. Isn't it (**cynical, feuding**) of you to ask other people to support a candidate in whom you yourself have no confidence?

13. One reason Coach Rawson is so popular is that he is firm and even tough with his players but never acts like a (**despot, bankrupt**).

14. Each answer will be considered right or wrong; no (**sagacious, partial**) credit will be given.

15. We will give careful attention to (**cynical, legitimate**) complaints, but we will not be influenced by silly faultfinding.

16. Your healthy body is a (**legacy, rite**) you have received from your parents, and you should strive to protect it from harmful influences.

17. A party that cannot offer new ideas to deal with the pressing problems of the day must be considered politically (**legitimate, bankrupt**).

18. No matter how efficient the new chairperson may be, the meeting will not proceed (**authoritatively, harmoniously**) unless the members cooperate.

19. During the winter, there are always a few (**partial, hardy**) souls who take a dip in the icy waters off Atlantic Beach.

20. Everything in life cannot be happy; we must expect some tears as well as (**legacies, mirth**).

Review Units 13–15

Analogies *In each of the following, encircle the item that best completes the comparison.*

1. sagacious is to **wisdom** as
a. stodgy is to breadth
b. bankrupt is to wealth
c. hardy is to endurance
d. ignorant is to knowledge

2. conqueror is to **vanquish** as
a. giant is to foster
b. despot is to oppress
c. impostor is to countenance
d. celebrity is to pall

3. hilarious is to **mirth** as
a. pedestrian is to novelty
b. wan is to splendor
c. resentful is to gratitude
d. nutritious is to nourishment

4. witch is to **enchant** as
a. impostor is to deceive
b. pedestrian is to cross
c. druggist is to heal
d. entertainer is to pall

5. impartial is to **prejudice** as
a. massive is to size
b. chronological is to time
c. cynical is to faith
d. authoritative is to obedience

6. handicraft is to **skill** as
a. gala is to daring
b. rite is to caution
c. feud is to intelligence
d. hoax is to cunning

7. meager is to **quantity** as
a. oppressed is to bulk
b. partial is to completeness
c. hardy is to stamina
d. gaudy is to brightness

8. legacy is to **will** as
a. definition is to dictionary
b. plot is to formula
c. character is to recipe
d. melody is to bill

9. hero is to **saga** as
a. judge is to romance
b. jester is to tragedy
c. detective is to mystery
d. villain is to comedy

10. reputable is to **patronize** as
a. honest is to grovel
b. shady is to boycott
c. fair is to haggle
d. untrustworthy is to countenance

11. cavalry is to **riders** as
a. artillery is to impostors
b. navy is to cynics
c. air force is to bankrupts
d. infantry is to pedestrians

12. harmonious is to **agree** as
a. feuding is to disagree
b. haggling is to agree
c. heeding is to disagree
d. clamoring is to agree

13. elongate is to **length** as
a. diminish is to width
b. coincide is to mass
c. inflate is to size
d. fluctuate is to height

14. sickness is to **indisposed** as
a. nervousness is to agitated
b. mirth is to afflicted
c. gratitude is to oppressed
d. boredom is to enchanted

15. maternal is to **mother** as
a. rural is to daughter
b. paternal is to father
c. fraternal is to sister
d. global is to brother

16. wan is to **color** as
a. cosmopolitan is to sophistication
b. reputable is to honesty
c. bankrupt is to money
d. brave is to courage

17. stodgy is to **unfavorable** as
a. cosmopolitan is to favorable
b. akin is to unfavorable
c. gaudy is to favorable
d. legitimate is to unfavorable

18. rite is to **officiate** as
a. trial is to hold
b. rally is to participate
c. appointment is to keep
d. meeting is to chair

19. miser is to **hoard** as
a. despot is to grovel
b. impostor is to haggle
c. bankrupt is to possess
d. spendthrift is to waste

20. saint is to **revere** as
a. victor is to vanquish
b. sage is to heed
c. thinker is to meditate
d. swindler is to obey

Identification   *In each of the following groups, encircle the word that is best defined or suggested by the introductory phrase.*

1. a meal that supplies what the body needs
a. nutritious   b. stodgy   c. hilarious   d. harmonious

2. carpentry, weaving, pottery, metalwork, etc.
a. pedestrians   b. handicrafts   c. impostors   d. galas

3. what a regular customer does
a. rob   b. serve   c. patronize   d. boycott

4. like a timetable
a. chronological   b. hilarious   c. gaudy   d. impartial

5. typical of a mother
a. akin   b. cynical   c. maternal   d. reputable

6. a plant that thrives even under unfavorable conditions
a. authoritative   b. massive   c. wan   d. hardy

7. property left to children by parents
a. haggle   b. legacy   c. vanquish   d. bankruptcy

8. prices going up and down rapidly
a. fluctuate   b. ignite   c. heed   d. diminish

9. the story of the adventures of a Viking like Eric the Red
a. hoax   b. saga   c. rite   d. gala

10. on a very large scale
a. chronological   b. massive   c. partial   d. sagacious

11. a loud outcry from angry people
a. gratitude   b. clamor   c. affliction   d. despot

12. used to be a lot of fun, but now we're tired of it
a. heed   b. transmit   c. pall   d. foster

13. exceedingly funny
a. chronological   b. impartial   c. hilarious   d. cynical

14. what a tyrant would do to the people he ruled
a. countenance   b. patronize   c. oppress   d. revere

15. birds of a feather
a. indisposed   b. akin   c. legitimate   d. hilarious

16. what a referee would do
a. coincide   b. officiate   c. meditate   d. hoard

17. laughter and merriment
a. feud   b. magnitude   c. affliction   d. mirth

Shades of Meaning   *Read each sentence carefully. Then encircle the item that best completes the statement below the sentence.*

Warned that the least agitation might cause the mixture to explode, lab technicians handled the container with extreme caution. **(2)**

1. In line 1 the word **agitation** most nearly means
    a. shaking   b. confusion   c. excitement   d. uneasiness

Evidence presented at the trial showed that far from being a "crime of opportunity" the burglary had been meditated weeks before. **(2)**

2. The word **meditated** in line 2 is used to mean
    a. reflected upon   c. discussed
    b. rehearsed   d. planned

The comedies of the Irish playwright Oscar Wilde are peopled with cosmopolitan types who speak in witty, glittering epigrams. **(2)**

3. The best definition for the word **cosmopolitan** in line 2 is
    a. global   c. sophisticated
    b. stock   d. international

To put maximum pressure on German defenses, the Soviet Army planned a massive assault on the Eastern front to coincide with the D day landings in Normandy. **(2)**

4. In line 2 the phrase **coincide with** most nearly means
    a. occur at the same time as   c. support
    b. fully agree with   d. draw attention from

It is true that his is a hard-luck story; but when will he learn that it is difficult to feel sorry for someone who grovels in self-pity? **(2)**

5. The word **grovels** in line 2 is best defined as
    a. crouches   c. cowers
    b. cringes   d. wallows

Antonyms   *In each of the following groups, encircle the word or expression that is most nearly **opposite** in meaning to the **boldface word** in the introductory phrase.*

1. oppressed the people
a. mistreated   b. reported   c. pampered   d. observed

2. ignite a match
a. extinguish   b. borrow   c. offer   d. light

3. a common **affliction**
a. experience   b. blessing   c. hardship   d. surprise

4. a **cynical** attitude
a. idealistic   b. bitter   c. stupid   d. intelligent

5. will **foster** their development
a. hold back   b. encourage   c. pay for   d. expect

6. reputable tradespeople
a. well-known   b. wealthy   c. local   d. shady

7. plan to **elongate** the hallway
a. shorten   b. clean up   c. clutter   d. decorate

8. enchanted by the story
a. pleased   b. ignored   c. surprised   d. disgusted

9. showed much **gratitude**
a. joy   b. heed   c. thanklessness   d. fear

10. revered the principle
a. invented   b. supported   c. honored   d. despised

11. a lifelong **feud**
a. quarrel   b. friendship   c. job   d. study

12. a **partial** summary of the book
a. complete   b. scholarly   c. written   d. unfair

13. made **sagacious** comments
a. brief   b. silly   c. wise   d. witty

14. felt **indisposed**
a. ill   b. unqualified   c. interested   d. healthy

15. failed to **heed** their warnings
a. obey   b. ignore   c. report   d. send

16. tried to **diminish** my reputation
a. equal   b. increase   c. confirm   d. lower

17. a **bankrupt** business
a. thriving   b. new   c. foreign   d. interesting

18. hoarded money
a. earned   b. amassed   c. paid   d. wasted

19. a **hardy** soul
a. kindly   b. generous   c. frail   d. sturdy

20. a very **meager** allowance
a. unexpected   b. lavish   c. useful   d. tiny

Completing the Sentence   *From the following words, choose the one that best completes each of the sentences below. Write the word in the space provided.*

Group A

handicraft	patronize	maternal	authoritative
legitimate	hoard	officiate	mirth
countenance	massive	nutritious	magnitude

1. Not until the storm died down did we realize the ＿＿＿＿＿＿＿ of the damage that had been done.

2. I may be only a lowly freshman, but I refuse to be _____ , even by the president of the senior class.

3. My _____ grandparents were both born in the United States, but those on my father's side of the family came from Italy.

4. She has been recognized by the United States and several other nations as the head of the _____ government of that country.

5. As a former college and professional football player, he is well qualified to _____ at our local high-school games.

6. Wasn't it foolish of you to expect a(n) _____ answer to your question from someone with no experience in the field?

Group B

blurt	**ignite**	**legacy**	**impostor**
cosmopolitan	**diminish**	**haggle**	**revere**
rite	**hilarious**	**pall**	**oppress**

1. Nothing you may say will lift the _____ of guilt and despair that hangs over him.

2. We were all in such a(n) _____ mood that it was almost impossible for us to take anything seriously.

3. In her will, my aunt left me a small _____ that I have put away for a "rainy day."

4. Anyone who claims to be an automotive engineer but doesn't know the first thing about car repair must be a(n) _____ .

5. I don't want to _____ , but at the same time I am not going to pay the ridiculous price that they are asking for the item.

6. The crowd was so excited that it seemed that any minor incident might be enough to _____ a riot.

Word Families

A. *On the line provided, write a **noun form** of each of the following words.*

EXAMPLE: sagacious — **sagacity**

1. harmonious _____

2. meditate _____

3. gaudy _____

4. meager _____

5. indisposed   _____

6. enchant   _____

7. fluctuate   _____

8. diminish   _____

9. authoritative   _____

10. inflate   _____

11. chronological   _____

12. hilarious   _____

13. ignite   _____

14. massive   _____

15. revere   _____

16. stodgy   _____

17. elongate   _____

18. impartial   _____

19. legitimate   _____

20. nutritious   _____

21. oppress   _____

22. transmit   _____

23. wan   _____

24. bankrupt   _____

25. coincide   _____

26. cynical   _____

27. hardy   _____

28. patronize   _____

29. partial   _____

30. officiate   _____

31. reputable   _____

B. *On the line provided, write a **verb** related to each of the following words.*

Example: indisposed — **indispose**

1. agitation   _____

2. affliction   _____

3. harmonious   _____

4. legitimate   _____

5. authoritative   _____

R

Filling the Blanks

Encircle the pair of words that best complete the meaning of each of the following passages.

1. The referee who _____ at a hockey game is like a judge presiding over a court of law. For that reason, he and his assistants must be as _____ as possible. If they show any favoritism in their calls, they'll hear about it from the fans.
   a. officiates . . . impartial
   b. agitates . . . authoritative
   c. clamors . . . cosmopolitan
   d. haggles . . . partial

2. "If we are to win this election," the Senator said, "we must put aside our private _____ and present a truly united front. Those who _____ this advice will be helping our cause. Those who ignore it can only hurt us."
   a. afflictions . . . diminish
   b. legacies . . . revere
   c. handicrafts . . . countenance
   d. feuds . . . heed

3. "I'm more than happy to shop at any establishment that is owned by a _____ businessman," Mom declared. "But I simply refuse to _____ a store that is run by people who are out to cheat me."
   a. despotic . . . bankrupt
   b. reputable . . . patronize
   c. cosmopolitan . . . foster
   d. legitimate . . . transmit

4. The tragic news of my best friend's death in an automobile accident cast a(n) _____ of gloom over our little gathering that evening and turned our _____ to tears.
   a. affliction . . . rite
   b. clamor . . . agitation
   c. saga . . . countenance
   d. pall . . . mirth

5. "I hate to _____ over minor details," the fussy little prince remarked to the court magician. "But as long as you're pulling things out of a hat, couldn't you come up with something nourishing? I'm hungry, and bouquets of fake flowers aren't particularly _____ ."
   a. haggle . . . nutritious
   b. meditate . . . massive
   c. grovel . . . pedestrian
   d. clamor . . . gaudy

6. "You certainly don't have to _____ your money like some miser would," I observed, "but if you continue to throw it around quite so freely, you'll soon be _____ ."
   a. transmit . . . stodgy
   b. hoard . . . bankrupt
   c. revere . . . pedestrian
   d. foster . . . indisposed

Analogies   *In each of the following, encircle the item that best completes the comparison.*

1. blindness is to **affliction** as
a. homicide is to ordeal
b. embezzlement is to catastrophe
c. pneumonia is to malady
d. perjury is to misdemeanor

2. legacy is to **beneficiary** as
a. oration is to speaker
b. gift is to recipient
c. turmoil is to firebrand
d. flight is to fugitive

3. impostor is to **counterfeit** as
a. notable is to prominent
b. fledgling is to proficient
c. braggart is to timid
d. parasite is to sullen

4. scurry is to **feet** as
a. mull is to legs
b. snare is to eyes
c. meditate is to ears
d. bellow is to lungs

5. quibble is to **haggle** as
a. foster is to stifle
b. entreat is to implore
c. grovel is to flounder
d. entice is to oppress

6. inflammable is to **ignite** as
a. graphic is to picture
b. unique is to prove
c. reluctant is to plan
d. insubordinate is to produce

7. farce is to **hilarious** as
a. overture is to literate
b. anecdote is to interminable
c. paradox is to quaint
d. tragedy is to heartrending

8. diminish is to **inflate** as
a. seethe is to capsize
b. enchant is to pamper
c. detest is to revere
d. consolidate is to abound

9. lamb is to **docile** as
a. cow is to sagacious
b. mule is to wayward
c. horse is to fickle
d. sheep is to regal

10. vindictive is to **vengeance** as
a. unscathed is to recompense
b. bewildered is to clarification
c. hospitable is to seclusion
d. cynical is to gratitude

Shades of Meaning   *Read each sentence carefully. Then encircle the item that best completes the statement below the sentence.*

Once exclusive to American cities such as New York and Chicago, skyscrapers have in recent years come to dominate many a European metropolis as well. (2)

1. In line 2 the word **dominate** most nearly means
a. control   b. eclipse   c. tower over   d. overshadow

Can you name the friar who officiates at the secret wedding of the doomed lovers Romeo and Juliet? (2)

2. The phrase **officiates at** in line 1 is used to mean
a. referees   b. conducts   c. moderates   d. chairs

My favorite painting in the exhibition was an Italian still life showing a pitcher, a fruit knife, and a bowl of mellow figs. (2)

3. The best definition for the word **mellow** in line 2 is
a. gentle   b. pleasant   c. ripe   d. rich

With the slogan "No taxation without representation!" American colonists protested the authoritative levies imposed by the British crown. (2)

4. In line 2 the word **authoritative** most nearly means
a. tyrannical
b. reliable
c. obedient
d. official

Although A.E. Glug tried many verse forms, he was partial to narrative poetry and indeed achieved his greatest success with the epic poem (2) *The Clodyssey* (1906).

5. The phrase **was partial to** in line 1 is used to mean
a. mastered
b. favored
c. was biased against
d. was trained in

Filling the Blanks   *Encircle the pair of words that best complete the meaning of each of the following passages.*

1. During the 14th century, the bubonic _____ , or "Black Death," suddenly swept across Europe, killing three quarters of the population and seriously _____ , or even paralyzing, the social and economic life of the continent.
a. goad . . . dominating
b. luster . . . inflicting
c. plague . . . disrupting
d. hearth . . . renovating

2. As I _____ idly through the curious book, my eye happened to light upon some interesting old photographs of haying and plowing and other scenes of life in _____ America at the end of the last century.
a. fluctuated . . . sodden
b. browsed . . . rural
c. tampered . . . gaudy
d. prescribed . . . radiant

3. I did everything I could to _____ them from pursuing a course of action that I firmly believed would end in disaster, but all my efforts were, unfortunately, _____ .
a. dissuade . . . futile
b. transmit . . . meager
c. mortify . . . spirited
d. swerve . . . disputatious

4. As the police officers who had been called to the scene of the accident were _____ eyewitnesses to the incident, a large crowd of curious _____ began to collect nearby.
a. lubricating . . . buffoons
b. procuring . . . dupes
c. patronizing . . . pedestrians
d. interrogating . . . bystanders

5. Though I admire the intrepid daredevils who _____ life and limb diving off towering cliffs into the sea, hundreds of feet below, I am much too _____ to try something like that myself.
a. hoard . . . hardy
b. hazard . . . timid
c. heed . . . stodgy
d. mar . . . lethargic

Final Mastery Test

I. Selecting Word Meanings *In each of the following groups, encircle the word or expression that is most nearly **the same** in meaning as the word in **boldface type** in the introductory phrase.*

1. a **foretaste** of things to come
a. criticism   b. result   c. anticipation   d. cause

2. **tamper** with the evidence
a. begin   b. interfere   c. agree   d. argue

3. received **innumerable** warnings
a. countless   b. threatening   c. official   d. detailed

4. an **animated** discussion
a. scholarly   b. dull   c. useless   d. lively

5. used all **available** employees
a. at hand   b. experienced   c. adult   d. qualified

6. commit **homicide**
a. embezzlement   b. theft   c. murder   d. lying

7. made a **fruitless** effort
a. strenuous   b. futile   c. unplanned   d. successful

8. made a **cynical** statement
a. poetic   b. long-winded   c. unnecessary   d. skeptical

9. **bewilder** one's parents
a. help   b. confuse   c. teach   d. please

10. **entreat** them to leave
a. command   b. beg   c. require   d. expect

11. an **anonymous** caller
a. dangerous   b. well-known   c. unnamed   d. angry

12. the **downtrodden** workers
a. well-paid   b. happy   c. skillful   d. oppressed

13. something that we **detest**
a. know   b. hate   c. welcome   d. understand

14. guilty of **perjury**
a. kidnapping   b. stealing   c. killing   d. lying

15. **capsize** the vessel
a. seize   b. overturn   c. purchase   d. repair

16. without any **incentive**
a. money   b. right   c. inducement   d. selfishness

17. a **cosmopolitan** point of view
a. mechanical   b. sophisticated   c. false   d. important

18. **gruesome** details
a. delicious   b. novel   c. horrifying   d. unexpected

19. a grueling **ordeal**
a. race   b. severe trial   c. setback   d. interview

20. made **lavish** preparations
a. hasty   b. careful   c. extravagant   d. stingy

21. left **ajar**
a. alone   b. partly open   c. untouched   d. sealed

22. where fish **abound**
a. leap   b. produce young   c. are protected   d. are plentiful

23. **foster** a new program
a. plan   b. object to   c. encourage   d. reexamine

24. an **impartial** decision
a. unbiased   b. lasting   c. hasty   d. prejudiced

25. start a **feud**
a. machine   b. quarrel   c. movement   d. alliance

II. Antonyms   *In each of the following groups, encircle the two words or expressions that are most nearly **opposite** in meaning.*

26. a. swerve   b. veto   c. maul   d. ratify

27. a. reputable   b. domestic   c. shady   d. humdrum

28. a. heed   b. decrease   c. officiate   d. accelerate

29. a. hostile   b. hardy   c. hilarious   d. heartrending

30. a. vital   b. leisurely   c. grueling   d. miscellaneous

31. a. remnant   b. bystander   c. regime   d. participant

32. a. graphic   b. injured   c. unscathed   d. pending

33. a. boycott   b. patronize   c. hurtle   d. grovel

34. a. quaint   b. puny   c. gigantic   d. orthodox

35. a. inflammable   b. cheerful   c. substantial   d. despondent

36. a. indifference   b. melancholy   c. narrative   d. enthusiasm

37. a. persist   b. reinforce   c. seethe   d. undermine

38. a. insinuate   b. entice   c. renovate   d. dissuade

39. a. enchant   b. presume   c. trickle   d. pall

40. a. spotless   b. ultimate   c. disputatious   d. grimy

III. Words in Context

In each of the sentences below, write in the blank space the most appropriate word chosen from the given list.

Group A

stifle	botch	potential	nub
dominate	meager	fledgling	impostor
nomadic	mull	malignant	flagrant
uncertainty	downright	inflict	interrogate

41. Although I realize you have lots of interesting stories to tell, I do wish you wouldn't always _____ the conversation.

42. When I was just a(n) _____ in my very first pro season, one of the veteran players took me under his wing.

43. Instead of giving me all those unimportant details, let's get right to the _____ of the matter.

44. He decided to give up trying to become a professional writer when he realized that his talents were really very _____ .

45. Only after I had _____ over the events of the evening did I realize how wrong I had been.

46. Though the situation in that part of the world is calm now, it is a(n) _____ powder keg that may go off at any moment.

47. It was _____ rude of her to ignore my kind offer of help.

48. Inexperienced as we were, we _____ the preparation of the meal so badly that we all had to go out to eat.

49. This mistake is so _____ that it cannot be overlooked, even though the manager's son was responsible for it.

50. With a great effort, I managed to _____ my anger and replied as courteously as I could.

Group B

adjacent	interminable	recompense	cache
implore	dilapidated	malady	elongate
transmit	iota	morbid	pamper
utmost	snare	preview	casual

51. The deserted cabin was so _____ that it looked as though any strong breeze would cause it to collapse.

52. Luckily, the communications officer was able to _____ an SOS signal just before the ship's radio went out of order.

53. Even though he lives in a house _____ to the school, he is often late for his first class.

FMT

54. In a tearful voice, the guilty man's wife _____ the court to treat her husband leniently.

55. The smile of joy she gave me when she received the award was ample _____ for all my time and effort in helping her.

56. He became hopelessly _____ in the web of his own lies.

57. Religious intolerance is a social _____ that simply cannot be countenanced in a democracy such as ours.

58. If you had a(n) _____ of consideration for us, you would turn down the volume on the TV.

59. The wait outside the operating room seemed _____ to the parents of the injured child.

60. When the younger players went in for the last few minutes of the game, we had a(n) _____ of what the team would be like next year.

IV. Words Connected with Moods

*The words in Column A may be applied to various moods that are typical of many people. In the space before each word, write the **letter** of the item in Column B that best identifies it.*

	Column A	Column B
_____	**61.** lethargic	a. sad, depressed
_____	**62.** peevish	b. filled with resentment or anger over something
_____	**63.** spirited	c. changing rapidly, especially in one's affections
_____	**64.** indignant	d. not caring one way or the other
_____	**65.** fickle	e. extremely cruel
_____	**66.** wayward	f. irritable, cross, easily annoyed
_____	**67.** vigilant	g. full of life and vigor
_____	**68.** indifferent	h. willing to forgive almost anything
_____	**69.** melancholy	i. on the lookout, alert
_____	**70.** docile	j. easily controlled and taught
		k. disobedient, insisting on having one's own way
		l. unnaturally sleepy or slow moving

V. Words That Describe Behavior

Some words that relate to the way people behave are listed below. Write the appropriate word on the line below each of the following descriptions.

dupe	parasite	insubordinate	lax
firebrand	prudent	poised	dynamic
fallible	inimitable	tactful	scrimp
regal	reluctant	proficient	vindictive

71. She is sensitive to the feelings of other people and careful not to hurt them.

_____

72. He expects to live off of other people.

_____

73. He dances in a way that no one else can equal or even try to match.

_____

74. She is so trusting that she is easily deceived and "used" by others.

_____

75. She shows great drive, originality, and ability to get things done.

_____

76. His speech aroused the fury of the mob.

_____

77. She saves every cent possible to help support her family.

_____

78. Like everyone else, she makes mistakes from time to time.

_____

79. He uses care and good judgment in handling his affairs.

_____

80. Hours of practice have made her a skillful pianist.

_____

VI. Word Associations

In each of the following, encircle the item that best completes the sentence or answers the question with particular reference to the meaning of the word in **boldface type.**

81. You would be most likely to **browse**
   a. in a library
   b. on the tennis court
   c. when you are asleep
   d. during a test

82. Which of the following suggests a person who is **frustrated?**
   a. "It's a great idea!"
   b. "Foiled again!"
   c. "I won!"
   d. "I'll do it!"

83. Which nickname would most likely be given to a **stodgy** person?
a. "Big Brain"
b. "All-American Boy"
c. "Stuffed Shirt"
d. "Miss America"

84. A person facing the **hazards** of life is
a. making money
b. taking risks
c. winning victories
d. playing golf

85. A person who receives a **legacy** has gained something as a result of
a. inheriting it
b. hard work
c. dishonesty
d. gambling

86. Which of the following would *not* be found in **rural** areas?
a. skyscrapers
b. water
c. cows
d. people

87. You would be most likely to **brood** over
a. an event of no importance
b. tomorrow's lunch
c. an exciting sports victory
d. failing an important examination

88. Which of the following would be most likely to create **havoc**?
a. a summer breeze
b. a game of volleyball
c. a school assembly
d. a tornado

89. Which of the following would *not* be likely to **canvass** an area?
a. an interviewer
b. a homebody
c. a pollster
d. a door-to-door salesman

90. Which of the following cannot be **quenched**?
a. a fire
b. ambition
c. a flood
d. thirst

91. An example of a **grim** event is
a. a birthday celebration
b. a fatal accident
c. a family reunion
d. a holiday

92. A customer gives a storekeeper a $1 bill that is seen to be **counterfeit.** The storekeeper will probably
a. accept it with thanks
b. offer $2 for it
c. refuse to accept it
d. donate the bill to charity

93. A person who **quibbles** during an argument is
a. winning the argument
b. splitting hairs
c. being courteous
d. getting angry

94. A **stalemate** lacks
a. a solution
b. a sense of humor
c. freshness
d. opponents

95. Which of the following is likely to be **sodden**?
a. a desert
b. a surprise guest
c. a rain-soaked field
d. a dust storm

96. If there is **mutual** admiration between Tom and Lynn,
a. the admiration is not genuine
b. they admire each other
c. the admiration is one-sided
d. the admiration won't last

97. Which of the following is *not* **transparent**?

a. a pane of glass

b. a feeble excuse

c. air

d. a wooden door

98. Memories that have been **eroded**

a. are still bright and clear

b. have been worn away by time

c. are painful

d. are set down in writing

99. A **braggart** would be most likely to

a. grin and bear it

b. stick to his guns

c. fly off the handle

d. toot his own horn

100. You would probably find it **mortifying** to

a. eat breakfast

b. earn enough money to buy your own clothes

c. win a dance contest

d. do poorly on this Final Mastery Test

Building with Word Roots

Units 1–3

pend, pens—to hang, weigh; to pay; to set aside

This root appears in **indispensable** (page 15), literally "not able to be set aside or done away with." The word now has the meaning "essential or necessary." Other words based on the same root are listed below.

dependent	**dispense**	**expenditure**	**perpendicular**
dispensary	**expendable**	**pension**	**suspense**

From the list of words above, choose the one that corresponds to each of the brief definitions below. Write the word in the space at the right of the definition, and then in the illustrative phrase below it.

1. at right angles; exactly upright, vertical _____

    stood _____ to the floor

2. a fixed amount paid to retired employees or their families _____

    received a small _____

3. the state of being uncertain or undecided; anxiety, nervous uncertainty _____

    kept us in _____

4. a place where medicines are made or given out (*"place from which things are weighed out"*) _____

    have the _____ fill the prescription

5. relying on another for help or support; determined or conditioned by something else; a person who is supported by another _____

    claimed two _____

6. replaceable, nonessential _____

    since no life is _____

7. to give out, distribute _____

    _____ justice with an even hand

8. amount of money spent; spending, using up (*"paying out"*) _____

    a list of all of our _____

From the list of words on page 131, choose the one that best completes each of the following sentences. Write the word in the space provided.

1. This tremendous project will represent an enormous _____ of public money.

2. In italic type the letters are slanted to the right, but in roman type they are

_____ .

3. Rescue workers set up a makeshift _____ , where medical supplies were provided to the survivors of the disaster.

4. A section of the bookstore in my neighborhood is devoted to novels of

mystery and _____ .

5. Whether or not we have our picnic tomorrow is _____ on the weather.

6. As the value of the dollar shrinks, Mrs. Persky finds it harder and harder to

live on the small _____ she receives from the government.

7. "Unlike human beings," said the captain, "supplies and equipment are

_____ since they can be replaced."

8. Because drugs can be dangerous, only trained pharmacists are licensed

to _____ prescription medicines to the ill.

Units 4–6

scrib, script—to write

This root appears in **prescribe** (page 41). Literally "to write before," this word means "to set down as a rule, order for medical treatment, or give medical advice." Some other words based on the same root are listed below.

circumscribe	**inscription**	**proscribe**	**subscribe**
indescribable	**postscript**	**script**	**transcribe**

From the list of words above, choose the one that corresponds to each of the brief definitions below. Write the word in the space at the right of the definition, and then in the illustrative phrase below it.

1. an addition to a letter written after the writer's name
has been signed _____

        add a(n) _____

2. handwriting; manuscript of a play or movie _____

add lines not in the _____

3. to sign one's name; to express agreement or
approval; to promise to take or to pay for _____

_____ to several hobby magazines

4. to draw a line around, encircle; to confine within
limits, restrict _____

_____ my after-school activities

5. to outlaw, forbid, prohibit; to banish _____

_____ all forms of exercise

6. beyond description _____

_____ joy

7. that which is written on a monument, coin, building;
a dedication in a book _____

read the _____ on the tombstone

8. to write out or make a typewritten copy of; to write
in another alphabet _____

_____ her shorthand notes

---

*From the list of words on page 132, choose the one that
best completes each of the following sentences. Write
the word in the space provided.*

1. We cannot _____ to a plan that would be unfair to so many
teenagers.

2. The dictator _____ all public meetings other than the ones
he himself ordered.

3. The director made several changes in the _____ to adapt
the play to a smaller cast.

4. Because I had forgotten to ask a key question in the letter, I added it as
a(n) _____ at the bottom.

5. The foreign language specialist _____ the Russian names
into our alphabet.

6. It is impossible to portray in words the way that the evening sunset filled

the sky with those _____ colors!

7. In 1519, the Portuguese navigator Ferdinand Magellan began a famous

naval voyage that eventually _____ the world.

8. The _____ in the book identifies it as a birthday gift my
father gave to his father 40 years ago!

Units 7–9

sist—to stand

This root appears in **persist** (page 64), literally "to stand through." The word now means "to continue firmly" or "to last." Other words based on the same root are listed below.

assistant	**desist**	**inconsistent**	**resist**
consistency	**exist**	**insistent**	**subsistence**

From the list of words above, choose the one that corresponds to each of the brief definitions below. Write the word in the space at the right of the definition, and then in the illustrative phrase below it.

1. to be, have life; to be real; to occur   _____

      _____ only in my imagination

2. to oppose; to exert force in opposition   _____

      unable to _____ the temptation

3. changeable, inconstant; not in agreement, contradictory   _____

      a(n) _____ performance

4. one who gives support or aid; a helper   _____

      a teacher's _____

5. continuing in a determined fashion; demanding notice   _____

      the reporter's _____ questions

6. to stop, cease to proceed or act; to discontinue   _____

      asked them to _____ from making that racket

7. the degree of firmness or stiffness; keeping to the same principles, habits, or level of quality   _____

      the _____ of whipped cream

8. the state of existing; a means of living or surviving; a living or livelihood; the minimum necessary to support life   _____

      _____ farming

BWR

From the list of words on page 134, choose the one that best completes each of the following sentences. Write the word in the space provided.

1. He showed occasional flashes of brilliance, but his performance lacked the _____ that is the mark of the true professional.

2. "It is our duty to _____ tyranny with all the resources at our command!" declared the speaker.

3. The defense attorney pressed the witness to explain why her testimony was _____ with the known facts of the case.

4. The parties in the dispute were ordered to _____ from making public statements while negotiations were still in progress.

5. The workers were paid a meager _____ wage that was barely sufficient to support themselves and their families.

6. We were awakened by a(n) _____ knocking at the door.

7. Many teenagers perform volunteer work as _____ in local hospitals, where they help nurses and orderlies perform their duties.

8. Do you believe that intelligent life _____ anywhere else in the universe?

Units 10–12

note, not—to know, recognize

This root appears in **notorious** (page 78), "widely and unfavorably known." Some other words based on the same root are listed below.

connote	**notary**	**noteworthy**	**notion**
denote	**notation**	**notify**	**notoriety**

From the list of words above, choose the one that corresponds to each of the brief definitions below. Write the word in the space at the right of the definition, and then in the illustrative phrase below it.

1. to indicate, be the sign of, mean exactly _____

   a temperature that _____ severe illness

2. to point out, give notice of, inform _____

   _____ us of their intention to sue us

3. an idea; a foolish idea or opinion; a small useful
item _____

     an odd _____

4. to suggest or imply in addition to an exact meaning   _____

     a name that _____ evil

5. remarkable, outstanding because of some special
excellence *("worthy of being recognized")*   _____

     a _____ remark

6. a record; a note to assist memory, memorandum; a
set of symbols or expressions _____

     add _____ in the margin

7. a public official who certifies statements and
signatures _____

     a _____ public

8. ill fame; being famous for something bad   _____

     achieve _____ as the leader of a local gang

---

*From the list of words on page 135, choose the one that
best completes each of the following sentences. Write
the word in the space provided.*

1. The typewritten deed became a legal document when it was signed by all
parties in the presence of a _____ .

2. The letter I received this morning _____ me that I had been
accepted at one of the colleges to which I had applied.

3. The flashing signals at the crossing _____ the approach of
a train.

4. What do you think was the most _____ achievement on
behalf of humanity during the past 25 years?

5. Isn't it fascinating how certain colors have come to _____
strong feelings, like red for anger or blue for glumness?

6. Place a _____ on her medical record card to remind the
nurse to send for her in two months.

7. All the _____ she had received after being a witness in the
bribery trial caused her to move to another city.

8. Do you have any _____ of what he is trying to do?

Units 13–15

rupt—to break

This root appears in **bankrupt** (page 110). Literally, the word means "bank broken," that is, "unable to pay one's debts." It also means "one who is unable to pay his or her debts" or "to ruin financially and thus make unable to pay debts." Some other words based on the same root are listed below.

abrupt **disruptive** **incorruptible** **irruption**
corrupt **erupt** **interrupt** **rupture**

From the list of words above, choose the one that corresponds to each of the brief definitions below. Write the word in the space at the right of the definition, and then in the illustrative phrase below it.

1. to burst forth (*"to break out"*) _____

_____ from the mouth of the volcano

2. a breaking; to break _____

a(n) _____ in the wall of the dam

3. to break in upon; to stop, halt _____

_____ her work to answer the telephone

4. a breaking or bursting in; a violent invasion _____

the _____ of the Goths into Italy

5. not open to immoral behavior, honest; unbribable _____

a(n) _____ public official

6. sudden, short, blunt; very steep _____

make a(n) _____ stop

7. rotten, wicked, dishonest; to make evil; to bribe _____

_____ the youth of the nation

8. causing disorder or turmoil (*"to break apart"*) _____

a(n) _____ development

From the list of words on page 137, choose the one that best completes each of the following sentences. Write the word in the space provided.

1. The bulkhead sprang a leak, causing a(n) _____ of sea water into the ship's hold.

2. Her unwillingness to listen to my side of the story caused a serious _____ in our friendship.

3. I know I shouldn't have _____ him in the middle of a sentence, but that sentence seemed as though it would never end!

4. The principal warned that the parents of _____ students would be sent for.

5. When cynics remark that "everyone has a price," they are expressing their belief that no one is truly _____ .

6. I was very much hurt when she made such a(n) _____ reply to my question.

7. The gamblers tried to _____ the athletes by offering them large sums of money to "throw" the game.

8. The police feared violence would _____ if the opposing groups of demonstrators were allowed to get near each other.

Index

The following list includes all the base words presented in the various units of this workbook, as well as those introduced in the *Vocabulary of Vocabulary* and *Building with Word Roots* sections. The number after each item indicates the page on which it is introduced and defined, but the words also appear in exercises on later pages.